Going All Out II

By

Dorian Sykes

RJ Publications, LLC

New York, New York

The characters and events in this book are fictitious. Any resemblance to actual persons, living or dead is purely coincidental.

RJ Publications
www.rjpublications.com

ISBN 10: 0981999867
ISBN 13: 978-0981999869

Printed in the United States

November 2011

1 2 3 4 5 6 7 8 9 10

Dedication

Adversity…..

I have grown to love you over the years, because you have been the one consistent thing in my life.

Acknowledgements

Ma' Dukes
From day one you have been the only one I could always count on. You have to forgive my impatience. I sometimes want things done too fast, but together we always seem to get there. And for that, I love you.

RJ Publications
I'd like to thank you all for allowing me to brand my own situation under yours. It really has been a motivation for me to continue writing.

Sha' Boggy
What's poppin' my nucca? You wanted part two, here it is. You be easy and stay up, shit gotta get better.

ATL Bobby
My workout partner. Where you at on your burpie game? My nucca, I hope you're somewhere doing better things and staying out the way.

D.C. Spree

By the time this hits the shelves you should be out of SMU and on the yard. Hold ya' head up and keep fighting. Things do change!

Prologue

"How's it going, Mr. Dickson?" asked Mr. Cunningham.

Pharaoh stared him down as the marshals removed his handcuffs and ankle bracelets. "What's all this?" asked Pharaoh adjusting his clothes.

"They just want to ask you a few questions. It'll be in your best interest to at least listen to what they're offering."

"Do you all mind if I speak with my attorney in private?" asked Pharaoh looking at the agents and prosecutor.

They looked at one another, shrugged their shoulders and reluctantly stood up and excused themselves into the hall. "I'm sorry about this" Mr. Cunningham said as the three walked out of the room.

"I thought I told you, I wasn't fuckin with these bitches. You hard of hearing?" asked Pharaoh.

"I'm simply looking out for you. They're threatening to file a superseding indictment because apparently you've been up there in Milan running your mouth."

"What the fuck are you talking about?"

"Some inmates, well informants, have debriefed with the government saying that you told them about your case; one of them is claiming to have bought from you in the past."

"And they can use this shit in court?"

"Can they? They'll use it to convict you beyond a reasonable doubt, and then some. I keep trying to tell you that this is the feds, not the state.

"I'm not a rat."

"Listen to you. I'm not a rat. Let me tell you something, in twenty years all that won't make a difference. Nobody will remember who told on who, let alone care. By the way, the government has offered to help you get your son back."

"My mom gone get my son."

"Not if the government has anything to do with it. Besides, do you want your son to grow up without his father?"

"What the fuck do they want from me?"

"For one, they want you to cooperate against Toro. And two, the murder Tez supposedly committed."

"And what do I get, besides the label of a rat?"

"I can guarantee you'll have some daylight."

"Nah, you got to come better than that if I'ma tell on the Mexican connection and homicide. Ya'll at least got to give me a ballpark figure."

"Hold on" Mr. Cunningham said as he raced into the hall.

"He's cracking, but he wants a ballpark figure" Cunningham explained to the agents.

"Richard, you know the law prevents us from making specific deals. How much time he receives depends solely on the judge," Agent Kemp said.

"So, what do you want me to tell him?" asked Cunningham.

"Tell him that we can put him in the guideline range of 144 months to 180 months if he cooperates fully. But it'll be up to the judge to depart any further from there," the U.S. District Attorney replied.

Mr. Cunningham raced back into the room, running his fingers through his thinning salt and pepper hair as he closed the door behind him. "Twelve to fifteen years," he said.

"Nope, not going to happen," Pharaoh mumbled.

"Hold on, I wasn't finished. They're offering twelve to fifteen years on the guidelines. They'll also file a motion prior to sentencing saying that you've cooperated substantially and the judge will have to start at the low end of the guidelines, then give you a time cut. In your case, the low end is twelve years, so he'll have to go below twelve. He can let you walk, once the government files the motion."

"All that shit sounds good, but I lost all interest when you said discretion, that means if he wants to. I'm straight on all that rat shit. I just wanted to see how them Yankees was coming. By the way, you're fired Pharaoh said, mocking the legendary Donald Trump.

Mr. Cunningham turned beet red. He tried to say something, but his words wouldn't come out. He stormed out of the room to relay the news. Pharaoh took a seat and smiled. He knew that there was a possibility he wouldn't ever see the streets again, but he could live with that so long as he had his dignity. "It's all or nothin'…" said Pharaoh.

Chapter One

Pharaoh sat nervously at the defense table, tapping his feet against the leg of his chair a million miles per second. He ate away at his thumb nail until tasting the salty taste of blood on his tongue. Pharaoh was a nervous wreck. It was jury selection day, and so far things were not going as his new mouthpiece, Ari Bailey, had promised. The U.S. Assistant Attorney, Ms. Francis Lee Carlson, had managed to strike all the potential black jurors with the exception of one. He happened to be the worst of all the jurors, a retired police chief for some small hick town not even listed on the map.

Pharaoh shook his head as the selection neared closing. He fought the urge to loosen his tie; he didn't want to seem any more nervous than what he already was. His stomach did a back flip and rested somewhere near his ass; the knot that was forming was brewing into a nervous fart. 'Fuck it,' thought Pharaoh. He loosened his tie and reclined in his chair, showing complete disdain for the jurors and the judge who was rattling on about trial would commence in the morning, and for the jurors not to be late.

"How could you let this happen? I don't stand a chance" Pharaoh growled as he grabbed a hold of Mr. Bailey's arm and squeezed tightly while looking him in the eyes.

"I think we made out well" Mr. Bailey replied nonchalantly.

Pharaoh smacked his lips and pushed Mr. Bailey's arm away. 'Lying mothafucka ain't do nothing he promised he would. Once he got that money, that $100,000 retainer, it was whatever happens' he thought to himself.

"We'll be fine." Mr. Bailey leaned forward in a whisper tone of voice.

Pharaoh wasn't trying to hear that shit. It wasn't about the money, his life was riding on this. It was all or nothin' for real. Pharaoh took one last look at the jurors and shook his head. Eight crackers, three Hispanics and ole' top cop – black ass. He didn't stand a snowball chance in hell. Pharaoh was prepared though, he had another plan. He knew something like this would happen; the prosecutor succeeded in selecting a fucked up jury. She selected people who weren't even from Detroit, who lived in small sub-divisions and who weren't exposed to the shady dealings of crooked cops and bad faith prosecutors. Every last one of those bastards believed that the government was their friend and was set up to protect them from thugs like Pharaoh.

The jurors looked down their noses at Pharaoh with a look on their faces that said "Nigga, you's guilty as charged." It was just a matter of going through the motions of a trial, but the verdict was already in: guilty! U.S. Assistant Attorney Carlson walked over to the defense table and set a witness list down in front of Pharaoh. She pulled back with a closed grin, then spun on her heels. Pharaoh flipped through the three pages of government rats set to lie and spill their guts at trial. There were twenty-two names altogether, only six of which Pharaoh actually knew. The rest were members of 'Let's Tell Something Records', them lying rat-face ass niggas who jumped on Pharaoh's case while he was in FDC Milan. The rest of the witnesses were car dealers and other people the government pressed to testify. Pharaoh found the one name he was looking for way down at the bottom of the list, Tez.

There it was in black and white, no denying it. Tez was their star witness. He had sold his soul to the devil himself. All this time Pharaoh refused to believe it, giving his best friend the benefit of the doubt, but it was true…Pharaoh closed the list and put it in his pocket. Tears started to well deep in his soul, boiling their way up to his eyes, but he fought them back. Francis Carlson reappeared, but this time she was carrying a stack of papers. She let the heavy stack slam down in front of Pharaoh. Her closed grin opened into a full-fledged Chucky E Cheese smile. Chinese bitch was grinning from ear to ear like her ass-hole was tickled pink. She managed to tell Pharaoh "this is your last chance to do something for yourself, and for the people seated behind you. Tomorrow, all deals will be off the table." "Listen, you dog-eatin' rice patty bitch" Pharaoh began, his voice rising with each word. "The deal's off the table already!" he shouted, and shoved the Rule II plea agreement off the side of the defense table.

Papers scattered everywhere, all over Ms. Carlson's feet. The small ruckus had gained the attention of the entire courtroom. Mr. Bailey put his arm between Pharaoh and Ms. Carlson, then spoke. "Ms. Carlson, we're not interested in any deal. We'll see you tomorrow at trial." Mr. Bailey tried smiling at the jurors whose foreheads were in wrinkles. "What are you doing, Mr. Dickson? Do you want the jury to have a negative perception of you before the trial even starts?" whispered Mr. Bailey.

"They already got a negative perception, that's why ya'll picked 'em." Pharaoh brushed Mr. Bailey's arm away from him. He was furious that Ms. Carlson would even have the nerve to trot her Chinese ass over and say this was his last chance to help himself, and then to top it all off, she brought his family into it like she really cared about their well-being.

After Judge John Corbett O'Meara finished his instructions, two U.S. Marshals rushed over to cuff Pharaoh. They wanted to leave the jury with the impression that Pharaoh was a very dangerous man. These were all premeditated tactics by the government. Anytime they were looking to railroad somebody, out came all the dirty games.

"I'll see you over at the jail tonight, so that we can prepare for trial in the morning," Mr. Bailey said. He was stuffing all the frivolous papers into his brief case.
"Don't bother" Pharaoh told him, then looked over at the prosecution table. Those devils had a plan for his ass, but Pharaoh had a plan of his own.

The Marshal gave Pharaoh a nudge in his lower back, as to say "get moving." He stepped through the small, wooden swinging door, which separated the defense table and rows of spectators. Pharaoh pulled back a closed smile at the sight of his only two reasons to fight, breathe, and exist. Ma' Dukes held Jr. in her arms, while waving his little hand. "Say hi to your daddy." "Hi daddy," said Jr. That almost killed Pharaoh, hearing his son's voice and seeing him for the first time in months. The Marshals ushered him out of the courtroom as if he were a terrorist. They had the silver U.S. Marshals transport van waiting on him as soon as he stepped off the elevator. Pharaoh was shoved inside while two Marshals got in and pulled out of the underground tunnel with a chase car at its bumper. Within minutes Pharaoh was back at the Wayne County Jail. Along the way he prayed that wouldn't be his last ride through the city,
'cause if tomorrow came and things went the way Ms. Carlson planned, he would die in a United States penitentiary. He shook the lingering thought from his mind, as the Marshals walked him through the garage tunnel into registry. They passed Pharaoh off, along with his paperwork for court, to Deputy Hanson.

"You ready to get upstairs, my man?" asked ole' Hanson. He was the coolest deputy working in all of Wayne County.
"Yeah. The sooner the better," answered Pharaoh.
"Bad day in court, young blood?" asked Hanson, as he led Pharaoh around to the change out room.

"Something like that."
"Well, I'ma tell you something," Hanson said before looking around the change out room. "Never let these honkies see you sweat, even if you are scared. Never give 'em the satisfaction of knowing it."
"That's real shit" Pharaoh said. He quickly changed from his blue power suit into his musty faded green county khakis.
"Take a few of these, maybe they'll help ease some of the stress." Hanson held out an open pack of Newport 100's.
"Good lookin', old head." Pharaoh didn't smoke, but he took a few just for the gesture.
"Who you callin' old? I bet any amount of money I could still take yo' ass out there on the court. I'ma have to come up to yo' unit and show you young boys how it's done." said Hanson. He had this crazy cool strut where his hand dangled to the side like an old pimp. "Come on" he said to Pharaoh.

He personally escorted him over to the annex building, all the while talking cashmere shit. With the current events of the day, Pharaoh needed the smile ole' Hanson provided. For some reason, listening to Hanson talk let Pharaoh know everything was going to be alright.
They came up on the sixth floor, and as soon as the elevator door screeched opened, Stacy stepped forward. "Thank you, Hanson, I can take 'em from here," said Stacy, taking hold of Pharaoh's arm and floor card.
"Don't thank me now, thank me later." Hanson said, shooting his shoot.
"You are a silly mess." Stacy slapped Hanson playfully on the arm as he back stepped onto the elevator.
"You could've gave the old nigga some rhythm, I wouldn't have gotten mad" Pharaoh joked as they started down the hall.
"I bet you wouldn't."

Stacy looked up and down the hall, then stopped. She reached for the mop closet door handle and shoved Pharaoh inside. She closed the door behind her, and leaned against it with sheer lust in her eyes. Pharaoh pulled her to him by the waist and let his hands travel up to the sides of her face, guiding their wet passionate kiss. Stacy reached her hand down inside Pharaoh's pants and found what she was looking for. She thought about it first when she rolled out of bed that morning, carrying her thoughts into the shower, but told herself she could hold off until later when they met for their secret tryst. Stacy stroked Pharaoh's rising dick while still kissing him.

"That's enough." Pharaoh pulled away from Stacy. They both were out of breath.

"I haven't had enough," Stacy said, trying to pull Pharaoh back to her steaming body.

"Later. We need to go over this, so there won't be any slip-ups. Is everything in place and ready?" asked Pharaoh.

"Yes. How many times do we have to go over this?" Stacy smacked her lips she wanted some dick and needed it in her life.

"We gone go over it until we know it's right, 'cause we only got one chance to get it right. Now, where's my stuff I asked you for?"

"I have it put away. Baby calm down, my end of things is taken care of" Stacy said, trying to assure Pharaoh. She wrapped her arms around his waist, then stole a kiss trying to spark back up where they left off, but Pharaoh removed her hands. His mind was racing a million miles per second. This had to work.

"I'ma go get ready."

Stacy rolled her eyes and blew out a breath of frustration, then turned the door knob. Stacy peeked her head out of the closet "come on" she said, seeing that the hallway was clear. She escorted Pharaoh down to his unit and popped the bars to let him in. All shit talkin', card playing, TV watching, workout routines, and even the shower ceased when Pharaoh stepped through the bars. Everyone had concern on their faces. Pharaoh was the O.G. of the block. He made sure everyone was straight; if you didn't have money for commissary, Pharaoh put money on your books, so you could make store. He made it possible for them to smoke all the weed and drink all the liquor they wanted. Pharaoh ordered pizza, shrimp, subs, chicken, Chinese food, – you name it, every night and he made sure the deputies brought enough in for everybody. So, quite naturally niggas were concerned. He was the life-line…

"What's up O.G., what they talking 'bout at court?" asked Terry.

"Ain't shit. We picked the jury today trial 'pose to start tomorrow" Pharaoh explained. He had everyone's undivided attention.

"You think you gone beat it?" asked Dusty.

"God willing, yeah." Pharaoh pulled back a smile to let his men know that he was holding up strong even though doubt lingered in the pit of his stomach. "Here, I got something for ya'll" he said, digging inside his sock. He tossed the four Newport 100's to old man Dusty.

Dusty's eyes lit up like he just hit the lotto. All the tobacco smokers gathered around Dusty, standing over his shoulder.

"Damn, get up off me," Dusty growled.

"You heard 'em P, said it's for all of us. Break bread old nigga," Trill demanded.

Pharaoh smiled and walked down to his cell. Once inside he put a sheet over the bars to provide some form of privacy, then he dug his arm through a small hole on the side of his mattress and felt around until his hand bumped the side of his Nokia pre-paid cell phone. He pulled the phone out by its antenna, then stretched out across the

mattress. He scrolled down to his lil' man Ralph's name and pushed send.
"What up doe." Ralph answered on the second ring.
"Tell me we all good."
"I got this triple O.G."
"So, everything's a go?"
"It's a go, green light, right-away, all that other shit too. I keep telling you that I'm on business. Relax."
"I know, but it's hard to. This shit has gotta work, or I'm fucked. All that planning for nothing."
"I got you, P. Stop talking negative shit up. I'm waiting on you and counting on you."
"Thanks Ralph. I needed to hear that. I'll see you in a minute. I think that's them calling my name for a visit."
"In a minute." *Click*

Pharaoh stood up and scanned the cell one last time before snatching the sheet down.
"Dickson, visit!" yelled Stacy. Pharaoh tucked the cell phone into the waist of his pants, then snatched the sheet down. He stepped out of his cell and gave all his men a play on his way out. Stacy stood waiting at the bars with her hands on the controls. She popped the gate to let Pharaoh out, and then walked him to one of the attorney-client visitor booths. "Look over in the corner" Stacy said, closing the sliding gate behind Pharaoh. "Hurry up and change. Give me your greens" she told him. Pharaoh handed Stacy his cell phone, then undressed in record time. He put his county greens in the bars, then reached for the black duffle bag which sat tucked in the back corner. He slid into Evisul jeans, pulled the crispy white –T over his head and stepped into the low-top white Air Force Ones. "Hurry…." Stacy said looking around. Pharaoh stood up after lacing his shoes and brushed his clothes. "Here" Stacy said, handing Pharaoh a visitor pass with someone else's name on it. She quietly slid the gate open, then unlocked the visitors door.

"Later." Pharaoh said, before leaning in to kiss Stacy. "Go…" she said, ending the kiss. She watched as Pharaoh disappeared onto the elevator. Pharaoh looked up at the numbers as the shaft lowered past each floor. He took a deep breath. When the door slid open he stepped off the elevator.

The only thing standing between him and his freedom was a metal detector and an old grey haired man perched behind the visitation booth. The corporal looked over the rim of his ancient gold glasses at Pharaoh. "Pass" the corporal said flatly. Pharaoh unfolded the pass as he approached the booth. He was hoping the old timer was one of Stacy's people. Pharaoh handed the pass to the corporal and tried to appear normal. "What are you waiting on? the corporal asked, looking up from the pass. "The world is waitin' son." Pharaoh managed to nod through the nervousness. "Be careful out there" the corporal said to Pharaoh's back, as he walked through the metal detector and out the door.

The warm afternoon sun shone down on Pharaoh's face as he stood outside the Wayne County Jail. That had to be the best feeling in the world, not Christmas, Thanksgiving, or your b-day, but one's freedom; liberty to do whatever the hell you please. Pharaoh closed his eyes and took in a deep breath of the city's thick air. *Honk! Honk!* Pharaoh opened his eyes at the sound of a car horn. He looked across the street at this triple black DTS Cadillac. Ralph rolled down the driver's window and stuck his yellow face out revealing his somewhat crooked teeth.

"Let's ride my nigga," said Ralph.

Pharaoh broke into a power walk crossing the street. He pulled on the back door handle and climbed inside the back seat, sinking into a plush leather seat. "What up doe?"

"Waitin' on you. I told you the shit was gone work. I got everything from Ma' Dukes, so we're all set" said Ralph.

"Good. Now pull off," ordered Pharaoh. He took a final look at the county jail and vowed never to return.
"You next" he said under his breath, talking to his man, Ollie, who was still on lock. Pharaoh kicked back and smiled. He couldn't wait to start putting his plan to work. It was all or nothin'

Chapter Two

"Can you see over into the city good?" asked Ralph. "Too good" answered Pharaoh. He was looking through a pair of binoculars over into downtown Detroit. Ralph and Pharaoh were standing on the back deck of his waterfront estate over in Windsor, Canada. Ma' Dukes purchased the property while Pharaoh was on lock; it was part of his escape plan. Windsor, Canada borders Detroit. The only thing separating the two is about a mile wide of water, known as the Detroit River. The two are so close that you could see cars riding down Jefferson Avenue even without the binoculars.

"Here, take a look" said Pharaoh, handing Ralph the binoculars. It was killing him not being in Detroit, but it was better than being on lock for the rest of his life. Pharaoh hung his head and thought about the task ahead of him. It seemed daunting and almost impossible, but it was his only plan, and it had to happen if he were to ever get his life back.

"What's wrong, P?" asked Ralph.

Pharaoh raised his head slowly. "This shit is just getting started." Pharaoh started toward the house.

"All you gotta do is give me the word, and it's done my nigga" Ralph said, eager to prove his loyalty. He followed Pharaoh into the house through the patio door, into the gourmet kitchen. Pharaoh walked over to the stainless steel double door Viking refrigerator and pulled out two bottles of Cristal. He set one down on the marble countertop of the island where Ralph sat perched on one of the stools. Pharaoh popped both corks, then pushed a bottle toward Ralph. "What we drinkin' to?" asked Ralph, raising his bottle of Crist.

"Hangover from last night" said Pharaoh, then he took a long swallow. He and Ralph hit Windsor's finest strip club that night, Daja Vu. They popped so many bottles that they didn't even remember coming home.
"Pharaoh, give me the plan. I know you already got some wild genius shit planned" said Ralph. Pharaoh turned around and reached for some papers hanging on the front of the refrigerator door by a magnet. He pushed the papers across the counter to Ralph.
"That's the plan" said Pharaoh.
"All these niggas is rats?" asked Ralph, looking over the three pages in front of him.
"Certified rats. You see what I put on the front of it."
"Hit list." Ralph read the red permanent marker, where Pharaoh scratched witness list out, and put 'hit list.'
"Tell me now if you can't handle it."
"P, I got you. All I need is these niggas address and we can start scratchin' names off the list."
"What do you mean we?"
"You know my crew is some head hitters."
"Yeah, but can they keep their mouth shut if they get knocked? We don't need to be staring at another witness list, feel me?"
"P, my niggas are tried, tested, and approved. I'm willing to put my life on it, that they'll hold up."
"And if they don't, it's yo' ass." There was a moment of silence; an awkward long moment of silence. Pharaoh took another swig from his now room temperature Cristal.
"Ralph, you know I got love for you like a son, but this is my life we're talkin' about here. It's not a game with me, so you need to be particular about how you take care of my business. And who you involve, feel me?"
"I'm tellin' you they're straight, but I get the point. It's on me," said Ralph.

"You see these names. All the ones with a target on them needs to be hit first, especially this one." Pharaoh flipped to the last page down to the last name.
"Tez," Ralph yelled.
"I know, it broke my heart too when I seen that, but it is what it is. Knock his head off too."
"Damn, that's fucked up…" Ralph flipped through the rest of the list, and counted using his finger to total the amount of names with targets on them. "Six" he said, stopping back on Tez's name.
"When you get back to Detroit go see Ma' Dukes, she's got something for you."
"So, let me ask you this my nigga, when all these niggas are put in the dirt, then…"
"Then, we can have our little trial. See, the government is ready waiting with a hammer in one hand, and a box of nails in the other. They can't wait to nail my black ass to the cross, but it ain't gone happen. We'll have a trial when I'm ready. And I won't be ready until all these rat-fucks are dead."
"So, you going to turn ya' self in?"
"Exactly. On some real life mob shit."
"I knew your ass had some ingenious shit cooked up. Don't them people know the worst thing they could've did was allow you time to sit up in there and think? And after all this is over with, what then?"
"Focus on this list. You already know I got us, all of us."
"I'm 'bouts to get in traffic right now" Ralph said, sliding down off the stool. "Can I keep this?" he asked raising the witness list.
"That's yours to keep. Just make sure you scratch the names off as you go." Pharaoh said, walking Ralph through the living room to the front door.
"What you gone do all day over here?" asked Ralph, stopping at the front door.

"Try not to die of boredom" Pharaoh said, and then he opened the door. He and Ralph stepped out on the huge wrap-around porch.
"Well, I'ma be over here from time to time. In the mean time O.G., triple O.G. you sit back and let me handle B.I. a'ight" Ralph said, extending his hand.
Pharoah pulled him in and they embraced with a half-hug and a slap on the back. "Be more than careful out there. Get it done, but don't rush nothin'" Pharaoh said.
"I got you" Ralph said, trying to give his O.G. a last minute reassurance.

Pharaoh watched Ralph to his car. He stayed on the porch until the Caddy became a small black dot cruising down the shoreline. "Damn," thought Pharaoh, stepping back inside the house. He shut the door and leaned up against it. Could Ralph really handle a task like that? Pharaoh knew he was asking a lot of his youngin'. He had just put the weight of the world on a 17- year- old's shoulders, and the crazy thing about it, Pharaoh knew that Ralph along with his little street team was about to really put that work in.

"You got all this shit started." Pharaoh said, talking to Tez as if he was standing before him. Pharaoh's mind wondered off back down memory lane when things were much simpler, before the money, cars, and dishonor. He managed to smile, as he remembered ever so clearly the time when Tez fought ole' crack head Cave Man; that shit was made for TV, a straight hood classic. One night while Tez was working inside their crack house he kept dozing off to sleep. Ole' Cave Man and some flea ass white bitch came over to buy some crack, and Cave man asked if they could use the back room to get high. Seeing as though the white chick spent $50 Tez went on and let them use one of the rooms, he figured the bitch had some more money 'cause the bill was crispy, like it was fresh out of the bank.

While they were back there beaming up to Scotty, Tez dozed off again. This time though, he didn't wake up until morning when Pharaoh came to check on him. The back door was wide the fuck open, all his drug money was gone, as well as his sack of rocks. Cave Man and his pink toe skank were also MIA. Tez jumped up and grabbed the one thing they hadn't taken, his 40 cal. from under the pillow he'd been laying on. "Come on. I know where they're at" he told Pharaoh, leading the way out the back door and down to James' house.

"He in there" said James, as if he knew Cave Man had done some dirt. "I knew his ass done stole somebody's shit, comin' round here with all that money and crack."

"You ain't say that last night when you was helping him smoke it all up," said Patty, another crackhead.

"I tell you one thing I'm not gone help him do, and that's receive that ass woopin' he got comin'."

Pharaoh and Tez dragged Cave Man out of the house onto the front porch. It was a struggle, Cave Man still weighed every bit of 280 lbs. and that was on crack. His old ass was not only strong as an ox, but he was also a hoot legend for knocking niggas out. Tez pushed Pharaoh back and told him not to jump in it. Cave Man stole the shit from him, so he wanted to be the one to handle his old ass. Plus, Tez wanted to dethrone ole' Cave Man of his knockout title. They squared off like two washed up fighters past their prime. Even though Cave Man stole Tez's shit, he still wasn't about to let him put his hands on him. "Come on young punk." Cave Man taunted while rocking back on his heels. The entire crackhead population within a ten block radius was out there cheering Cave Man on. They formed a circle around the two, while Pharaoh clutched the cold steel of Tez's 40 cal. Cave Man faked a jab, then caught Tez across the jaw with a quick two piece. Tez stumbled, but didn't fall. He wiped the back of his hand across his mouth smearing blood everywhere. The sight of his own blood infuriated Tez. He lowered his head and charged at Cave man only to be slung like a wet rag doll. Tez broke his fall and stood up. Deteremined to hold his ground, Tez squard off with ole Cave Man and boxed his old ass like a grown man would. He rolled with the punches and even tagged Cave Man here and there. They fought for all the five minutes, until the Detroit Police pulled up. Both of them were out of breath, ready to pass out. The police couldn't have shown up at a better time. Tez didn't win the fight, but he sure as hell didn't lose neither. He left as a man, with the respect of the hood. Pharaoh came back to reality. He shook his head and wondered what happened to the fighter he knew Tez to be, where did he go? The white man pull up with only some papers in his hand, and niggas lose all the fight in them, go from being gangsta's to something else. Snitches!

"There you are. I thought you forgot all about us," said one of the two blondes Pharaoh brought home from the club last night. She walked down the spiral staircase and over to Pharaoh.

"You miss me?" she asked in the most proper French accent.

"I did" Pharaoh said smiling. He was starting to recap last night's events, some of them anyway. He drank entirely too much to remember everything. Hell, he didn't even remember the stripper's name, or if he'd even bothered to get it. He was eager to see what the other girl looked like. If she was half as beautiful as the one leaning against his chest fondling his manhood, then ole' Canada wouldn't be so bad after all.

"Come on, let's go back to bed. Melissa is waiting on us."

"And what's your name?" asked Pharaoh.

"Jessica, silly." The girl laughed, then pulled Pharaoh away from the door leading him up the staircase.

Pharaoh enjoyed the view of Jessica's camel toe from the back. All she had on was a short T-shirt that fit her like a mini skirt. Melissa was sprawled out across the bed, still the way Pharaoh had left her, naked. "Look who I found," said Jessica. "Where have you been Mate?" asked Melissa. Her accent was just as strong as Jessica's. She rolled over onto her back totally unashamed of her pretty pink pussy with a blonde landing strip just above her clit. Melissa and Jessica both reached for Pharaoh, undressing him like two horny teenagers. Jessica shoved Pharaoh playfully into the bed, then crawled in after him. Pharaoh laid between them on his back with 10 inches of hard black dick standing straight up. Jessica and Melissa were fascinated by the size of Pharaoh's dick. They giggled to one another, like 'who's going to suck it first.' Melissa grabbed the base of it and put only the head in her mouth. She moaned, as did Pharaoh from the platinum Canadian head he was receiving. "Shit." He sighed, putting his hands behind his head, while Melissa looked up into his eyes. "Let me try" Jessica said, taking Pharaoh's dick from Melissa. They took turns giving Pharaoh head, both trying to be the one to make him skeet.

Pharaoh reached for the remote on the night stand. He clicked the TV onto Channel 4 News, and low and behold, U.S. Assistant Attorney, Francis Lee Carlson was holding a live press conference. Pharaoh smiled as they showed his mugshot, then a picture of his cell at the County Jail. They couldn't explain how he escaped, they just knew he was on the loose. "You ain't seen nothin' yet" Pharaoh said. Heturned off the TV and tended to Jessica and Melissa's fine asses.

Chapter Three

"What the fuck does any of this have to do with me? I don't give a damn about him escaping, ya'll need to catch him" said Tez. He was pacing his living room floor, listening to FBI Agent Kent ramble on…

"It's not me, Martez. Ms. Carlson wants us to keep a close eye on you until we can get Dickson back into custody" Agent Kent explained.

"What you mean, like sit outside my house all day?"

"Of course not. We're going to move you to another location somewhere safe."

"Some witness protection shit?"

"Sorta, you can call it that."

"All this high-powered rat shit wasn't in my deal. What if I say no?"

"Then, we put you in jail and hold you there until we catch Dickson and have his trial." Tez was already packing his suitcase. He figured Agent Kent was stalling him on the phone, all the while somebody was on the way to pick him up. "Martez, we're doing this for your own safety. We have reason to believe Dickson is going to come after you. Just go with the flow, two U.S. Marshals are on their way to get you, okay?"

"I hear you. I'll be here." *Click.*

Tez hung up the phone and scanned his bedroom making sure he hadn't forgotten anything. His suitcase was packed with handguns and assault rifles; what he called his tools. Tez zipped his suitcase shut and snatched if off the bed. He stormed through the hall into the kitchen and out the side door. Tez popped the trunk on his 600 SL, then tossed the suitcase inside. He briskly walked around the driver's side and climbed behind the wheel. As he turned the key the engine made a hissing sound, then winded down. It sound like he needed a timing chain. The gas light popped on the dash; joining the oil and brake light as well. When he shifted the car into drive a thick cloud of smoke engulfed the driveway. "Just make it to the gas station" Tez told the car as he pulled out. He stopped at the corner, then made an illegal turn down a one way side street, and made a left on Albany Street. Tez gave the car some gas and let it coast two blocks down to 7 Mile where he pulled into the Sunoco Gas Station on Syracuse Street. He parked at an empty pump then got out. The car ran out of gas and cut off before he even had the chance to turn the key back.

Tez noticed the afternoon ritual dice game popping near the air pump. Floyd, John, Pope, Pooh, Twan and Lemon Head all kneeled over totally oblivious to the killer lurking behind them. All them niggas were scared shitless of Tez. Even after it came out that Tez had snitched on Pharaoh and Ollie, niggas in the hood still showed him the same amount of respect as before, or fear for a better choice of words. Sure niggas were whispering behind his back, but one thing for sure whenever he came around it was all smiles. Not one of them had the heart to tell Tez to his face, "nigga, you's a rat and a coward." A rat he was, but a coward no. Niggas knew Tez was still crazy, despite rolling over, and they knew he'd still bust his gun.

Tez walked inside the gas station and stopped in front of the counter. He mean-mugged the Arab named Baby working behind the bulletproof glass. Baby had this look on his face that said, "Please, I don't want any trouble – just go." Tez strolled toward the coolers and snatched an orange Crush soda. He cracked it open and began drinking it as he walked back to the counter. He set the soda on the counter and wiped the beads of sweat from his forehead with the back of his hand.

"Let me get a box of Swiser's and twenty on pump two Tez. He picked up his soda and killed it. "Fuck you waitin' on?" he asked.

Baby didn't move a muscle. "For you to pay for these items," said Baby. "You still haven't paid for last fill up."

"Pay? Let me tell yo' Arabian knight ass something. If anybody's gone start paying it's gone be you and the rest of you terrorist mothafuckas. I let you sit on my corner and sell ya' little gas and cigarettes for years, and you talkin' 'bout pay. Niggas can't even sell they drugs on the corner without worrying about me taxing them, and yo' ass ain't no different."

"Please go," said Baby.

Tez pulled his 40 cal. from his waist and pointed it at the bulletproof glass. He turned toward the coolers and let off three shots, shattering two of the glass doors. He shot through some chips and toilet items, then spun back around to face Baby.

"Okay, okay. Just please don't damage anything else," pleaded Baby, as he punched Tez's gas into the register. He stuffed two boxes of blunts into the shoot, and continued to plead with Tez.

"A'ight. But let me hold fifty dollars to get in the dice game. I might give it back to you." Baby stuffed three twenty dollar bills into the shoot, and pointed for the door.

"See you tomorrow, Baby" Tez said, leaving as if nothing had happened. He tucked his 40 cal. back into his waist and walked over to the gas pump. He started the pump, then walked over to the dice game.

"What they hittin' for?" he asked.

"Ahh shit" John John said as he turned around to stare death in the eyes.

Pope, Twan, Floyd, and Lemon Head all started tucking money on the low. Tez was known to stick a game up in his day. In fact, just last week he robbed all them

niggas with no gun, made them all get naked and everything, and he'd come back the next day like ain't shit happened.
"Bet you miss." Tez said, talking to Pope who was on the dice. No sooner than Tez said that, Pope cropped out.
"Ole' janky ass nigga," Pope mumbled under his breath as he stood up.
Tez hadn't heard him, he was too busy reaching for the dice. He shook the dice high above his head. "What ya'll shootin'?" he asked.
"Twenty, forty. Something light," said Floyd.
"Well, I'm shooting' forty," said Tez.
"You got your back fade, Pope?" asked Floyd.
"Nah, you get 'em" Pope mumbled.
"Where yo' money at?" Floyd asked Tez.
"Nigga, since you worried so much about my money, put us both up. Mines and yours," ordered Tez.
Floyd looked at him like "is this nigga for real?" Knowing that Tez was serious as cancer, Floyd let four twenties float down to the cement.
"Dance bitches" Tez said, rolling the dice out. The dice twirled for a few seconds, then landed on seven.
"Shoot back" Tez said, picking up all the money.
"You gotta leave something down if you going back," Lemon Head said.
"And since yo' lemon meringue pie head ass so worried about the money, you put us both up" said Tez, as he shook the dice high above his head.
"You already know I'm not going for no shit like that" Lemon Head replied.
"What yo' bitch ass say, you ain't scared to talk to me like that?" Tez dropped the dice and started toward Lemon Head.
"I'm just saying. You always come through and fuck our game up," said Lemon Head.

"Come on, Tez. Let 'em make it" Twan pleaded.
"Matter of fact, here," Twan said, handing Tez forty dollars.

Pope, John John, Floyd and finally Lemon Head all followed suit, each giving Tez some bread. The death that lingered in Tez's eyes disappeared and a smile widened across his face. That's all his crazy ass wanted was to know niggas still had respect for him the in streets after he told on Pharaoh.

"Can we please get back to our game, Tez? We don't want no problems," Twan pleaded.

"Yeah, I'ma leave ya'll to ya'll game." Tez said tucking his money into his pocket.

John John gave him three bags of weed and sent him on his way. Them coward mothafuckas sighed with relief that Tez was leaving. The little money they each gave him was pennies compared to if he decided to flip out and just rob everybody.

Tez watched a navy blue Chevy Tahoe bend the corner heading in the direction of his house. There were two white men inside, both sporting dark shades. No doubt who they were. They were the two U.S. Marshals on their way to pick Tez up. He quickly started the Benz and waited for the winding noise to stop, then he peeled out the lot heading west on 7 Mile Road.

The further he drove the more clear it became to Tez that he didn't have anywhere to go. The streets wasn't fucking with him like that, he burned all his bridges, and he couldn't go to his mom's house cause that would be the first place the feds looked once they realized he was ghost. Tez was essentially homeless. With his back against the wall he knew exactly what he had to do in order to survive. It was easy – just turn up the heat and get back on his bullshit. Every nigga who looked like they was getting money had to pay. Tez knew exactly where he'd start first. He stretched out with one hand gripping the wheel, as he let the Benz coast down 7 Mile Road.

"Niggas 'bouts to feel the wrath" he said, pulling his 40 cal. from his waistband. He massaged his handle while continuing to scour the west side of Detroit. There would be no more petty stick-ups just for the sake of old respect. Each lick had to be a major score or Tez wasn't fucking with it. He told himself these things while rolling up one of the blunts. It was time to step out of Pharaoh's shadow too. Niggas still had Tez on some, "oh, that's Pharaoh's people," like he was a worker and not his own man. That shit always irked Tez on the low. Now was the perfect time to set his own legacy, and not just for being known to kill, but a real life gangsta.

Tez had a plan for how to erase the snitch label he wore on his back as well. All he had to do was find Pharaoh and kill him, then he wouldn't have to testify. Right now all the streets had was speculation, he said she said. 'Find him kill 'em' thought Tez, taking a pull from the blunt. "Yeah!"

Chapter Four

"Can I get you anything else, baby?" the butch- body bar maid asked Ralph for the fourth time.

"I'm good." Ralph told her with a half grin. He watched as ole' strong back turned and walked down the bar to serve another customer.

Ralph was perched on a stool at the far end of the bar. He chose that seat so he could watch the entire club, all the faces, and more importantly the front and only door. He baby sat the same piss warm Corona beer for over two hours, taking midget sips here and there, but that's not why Ralph was there. He was there to scratch the first name off Pharaoh's 'hit list.'

The name of the club was Outkast. It's an old dingy one way in -one way out death trap, known to the city of Detroit as the headquarters of the Outkast motorcycle gang. They used the club to hold meetings, but more so to throw wild shindigs. Tonight was no different. The dimly lit club was packed with Outkast members, its associates, and grey people such as Ralph who were just looking for a good time. Smoke clouded the air almost making it impossible to see every face. Women dressed in skin tight leather catsuits, filled a makeshift wooden dance floor. They were out there doing body shots and a bunch of other wild shit. If Ralph wasn't there on business, he would be right in the midst of all the leather and ass.

Ralph damn near knocked his beer over at the sight of Chris, his target. He dug in his pocket and looked at the picture twice and back up at Chris. Yeah, it was him. Chris came walking out the back of the club from some door Ralph hadn't noticed. He stepped behind the bar and shared some words and smiles with ole' butch-body.

Ralph pulled his cell phone from his hip and pushed the call button. "Yeah, the nigga is in here. He must've snuck past ya'll. He's wearing a black Dickie's outfit with a leather bandana around his head. Get in here before he disappears, he's behind the bar right now." *Click.* "That was Ralph" Swift said, closing his cell phone. He turned slightly in the passenger seat of the stolen Dodge Minivan to face his cohorts. "He say the nigga's standing behind the bar right now wearing a black Dickie's outfit and a leather bandana on his head. Tuff, Robin – I want ya'll to hit the door first. I'ma be right behind ya'll. All ya'll gotta do is make a way. J-Nutty, you just keep the engine running and yo' eyes and ears open," Swift told them.

Swift and Ralph were best friends and the top two of their five man crew. Swift got his name 'cause he was a little short, fat black nigga who was quick on his feet, with his hands and on the draw. So, niggas in the hood started calling him Swift. "Ya'll ready?" he asked. Without answering, Tuff and Robin slid out the side door of the van, stepping into the pitch black darkness of the warm summer night. They both put their black hoodies over their heads and fell in step crossing the street. Tuff and Robin were half brothers, sharing the same crackhead father. They looked so much alike that they told everyone that they were twins. It would save them the time and heartache it took explaining how both of their moms were strung out on drugs, and they were all each other had. They were closer than twins.

Tuff and Robin fell behind two obviously drunken women as they staggered out of the parking lot towards the entrance of Outkast. Both young black women laughed and pushed at one another until one of them saw the two dark shadows behind them.

"We ain't got no money" she said out of fear, while tapping her friend.

"Bitch, we can see that. We're going in the club," Tuff said.

"Who you callin' a bitch?"
"You bitch. Now turn around and knock on the door and shut up" snapped Tuff.

He and Robin nonchalantly, put their backs to the wall and waited while the two women pounded the steel black door with their fists. The sliding peephole could be heard as it scratched back against the metal of the door. Loud rave type music poured out of the hole, as did a stream of light. The slider closed and the music ceased. It was as if the Outkast was a fortress, soundproof doors, the entire building was spray-painted black and there were no windows; a death trap for sure.

The door slowly opened and the two women were allowed in. As the 7 foot bouncer tried to close the door, Tuff sprung from the side of the wall and hit him three times in the gut, then twice in the dome on his way down to the floor. Screams filled the club and people started for the exit, but Tuff and Robin were dropping them in their tracks. Ralph pulled his baby 380 from his nuts and leaped over the bar. He ran up to the butch bitch who was kneeled down trying to pull up a sawed-off double barrel shotgun. Ralph put her brains all over the empty shots glasses, as he shot her twice execution style. A shot glass exploded just inches away from Ralph, then another one. Somebody was taking shots at him. Ralph crouched down next to butch-body, using her lifeless body as a vest. He grabbed the shotgun and looked around. It was Chris licking shots off at him. Chris saw Ralph grab the gun and broke upstairs toward his office, but Swift was on the nigga's heels about four steps behind him. Swift stopped at the bottom of the steps and pointed his 30 cal. Desert Eagle up at Chris' back. Ralph watched as the cannon exploded, he could see the large shells ejecting from the gun as the shaft slid back with every burst. Fire, then smoke spit from the barrel at least four times. Swift lowered his gun to chest level and started up

the stairs, Ralph wasn't far behind. They found Chris lying on his stomach in a pool of blood at the landing. He had made it into his office, but couldn't close the bulletproof door in time. ..
"Roll yo' bitch ass over" ordered Swift, as he kicked Chris square in the ass. Chris made a groaning sound, then rolled onto his back. The 50 cal. slugs went through his back and came out his chest. "Look at me you half dead mothafucka," ordered Swift. He wanted Chris to look him in the eyes before he killed him.
"Fuck you" Chris managed. He knew that he was about to die, so why give these two young punks the satisfaction of him begging for his life.
"I got a message from Pharaoh, bitch nigga," said Ralph. He pointed the double barrel down at Chris's face. "I got this one" he told Swift.
"That's alright you ain't gotta look at me." Ralph said, pressing the two barrels against Chris' eyes. He shoved down hard then squeezed the trigger.

There was nothing left but a neck detached from a body. Chris' entire head exploded from the blast. His brain matter splattered all over his office and onto the clothes of Ralph and Swift. "Rat mothafucka" Ralph said, taking one last look at his work. He followed Swift back down the stairs to the club area. Tuff and Robin were at the bar having themselves a good ole' time. Everybody in the club was dead with the exception of the D.J. Tuff told him to play Jay-Z 'Hard Knock of Life' and put it on repeat.
"What the fuck is you two nuts down here doing?" asked Swift.
"No bullshit," laughed Ralph.
"Shit, pull up and have a drink. The bar's on me tonight" Tuff joked.
Robin was playing bartender. "What ya'll want?"
"I'm straightt" Ralph said.

"Me too" added Swift.
"Well, pour me another round and give this bitch beside me whatever she wants" Tuff said, lifting the head of the chick he cussed out on the way in. She was dead as E-mothafucka.
"Come on, we out" laughed Ralph, as he started for the door.
"What about all this liquor and shit?" asked Tuff.
"I'll buy you some, whatever you want, lets just get outta here" Ralph demanded.

Tuff and Robin still grabbed all the Henny and Remy Martin they could carry. They had already gone through the pockets of all the dead bodies and raided the cash register. Ralph stepped out into the night and pulled his cell phone from his hip. He scrolled down to Pharaoh's name and texted these words '1 down.' They all piled inside the stolen van and went to Coney Island to get something to eat, then to the crib to play NBA Live '03 on Playstation 2. For the young wild bunch, murder and robbery is what they specialized in, living strictly off the land. Not one of them had a hustla's bone in their body. They stayed broke, it made them easier to provoke, living from day to day, lick to lick. All they had was each other. All of their parents were crackheads. So, they were forced to survive and they would do so by any means.

Chapter Five

The jux Tez had planned yesterday was a complete dummy mission. He robbed this Westside nigga by the name of Pac Man, who was supposed to be holding, turns out that Pac Man was just the middle- man. Tez hooked up with him at Starter's Lounge, and told him that he wanted to buy a half brick soft. All the while, Tez was thinking that Pac Man had the coke, but when they made the transaction Pac Man didn't have shit. He was to count Tez's money then take it back around the corner while skimming a few thousand off the top for setting up the deal. Tez ended up shooting Pac Man in the stomach twice for wasting his time. He pushed him out of the car onto the pavement of Starter's dingy parking lot.

It was back to the drawing board. Tez spent the night in his car and was set on never doing so again. He was starting to get musty and his breath stunk. 'This shit can't go on' Tez told himself as he scowered West 7 Mile Rd. in search of a jux worthy of his gangsta. Tez's eyes lit up when he saw this nigga named Dale he went to school with. He had heard how good Dale was supposed to be doing. Word on the street was that Dale got out of the game and now had four car dealerships spread throughout the city, Southfield Expressway being his main location. Dale walked side by side with some woman down the row of exotic cars which filled his lot. He talked with his hands describing each car and its luxury. Tez parked on the side street, and walked around the gate into the lot. Dale was saying something to the woman in a last effort to sell her a car. He waved his hand at the back of her head. "If you lookin' for a bargain try Mel Farr" Dale suggested.
"What up doe" Tez said.

Dale tucked his head back and studied Tez's black face and bald head. It had been a minute since they'd seen each other. "Tez?"
"Yeah, nigga don't act like you too rich to remember a mothafucka."
"Same ole' Tez. Give me some" Dale said, extending his hand.
"It's been what, fifteen years?"
"Bout that long. I heard you were doing your thing, how's business?" asked Tez.
"I'ma tell you like I tell all the other brothers I came up with in the game. Leave that game alone as soon as you can afford to. Do what you gotta do to get where you tryna' get, then call it quits. Problem is most of us don't know where we tryna' go. But business is great! These white folks gave me the blueprint and ain't no way I'm lookin' back."
"I feel that. I see you got the latest whips."
"Yeah, all we carry is exotic cars." Dale pointed to the sign mounted high above the dealership.
"Why, you shoppin' for something new?"
"Yeah, what's this silver thang staring at me?" I'm likin' how bulky it is."

Dale walked Tez over to a new Audi A8. He opened the driver door and stood back, letting Tez climb behind the wood grain steering wheel. Tez fell in love with the car and he hadn't even driven it yet. The fine Italian cut leather upholstery and the wide bucket seats made Tez feel like he was on a boat and not in a car.
"How much?"
"Ha" laughed Dale. "You're not serious are you? I know you just didn't have the balls to ask how much. Come on, out" Dale said waving Tez to get out of the car. He had already wasted enough time for the day on ole' girl's window- shopping ass.
"I'm talkin' about on a trade-in for my 600."

"Where's it at?" Dale asked, looking around. He spotted Tez's black 600 SL parked across the street. "Go get it and we'll see what we can work out." Tez went to pull his car around and into the lot. When Dale saw the aged Benz he put his hand over his mouth and laughed. Tez jumped out leaving the engine running.
"Tez, I can't do nothin' with this car."
"Why not?"
"For one it's a dinosaur. And two, it sounds like it's got more problems than me."
"Tune up, oil change, and maybe a paint job and this boy's back in the game" Tez smiled.
"I can't put this on my lot. People a swear I'm sellin' lemons."
"Well, what kind of deal you gone give me without a trade-in?"
"You give me fifty thousand, and I'll put you in the Audi today, rims included. Of course you'll owe me another hun'd grand financing."
"Shit, I got that right here in the trunk."
Dale rubbed his hands together like the greedy bastard he was. "Then, I guess we have ourselves a deal."

Tez popped the trunk and pulled out his suitcase. Dale ushered him inside the dealership like he was the president himself, all while barking orders to his secretary. "I want the keys and the Bill of Sales, drawn up for the new Audi out there. Put it in the Johansen name." Dale walked Tez inside his office and waved for a seat while he peeled out of his suit jacket. Dale went straight to work, grabbing the phone and stuffing papers into his fax machine. Tez watched Dale finagle financing for the deal and send the papers off, then receive them back. He wondered just how much money Dale was making doing this, and where he kept it.

"Yes. I'll have your end for you in the morning" Dale said, then hung up the phone. He shuffled some papers around on his desk.
"Everything looks to be in order; we're just waiting on your keys and paperwork. Your note will be two grand, insurance included. Stop by tomorrow and I should have your plates, you can use this for now." Dale handed Tez a 14 day temporary sticker.
"Okay, now all we gotta do is count that money out." Dale did a drumroll with his fat yellow fingers and focused intently on Tez as he unzipped the case. Dale's back glued to the chair and his face registered with absolute fear when Tez came out the case with a short stock AR-15.
"What's…what's going…on?" stuttered Dale.
"Smooth open" Tez said calmly.
"And what's… smooth open?"
"Smooth open the safe, before I smooth open yo' shit." Tez cocked the AR back, letting a gold 223 shell slide into the chamber.
"I thought we were cool."
"Bitch nigga, we ain't never been cool. Get up and open the safe!" yelled Tez.
"Okay. Please just don't kill me." Dale stood up and back stepped over to a manila colored file cabinet. He kept his eye contact with Tez, so he'd know that he wasn't trying anything. Dale pushed the cabinet to the side, revealing a safe built into the wall.
"Open it" ordered Tez.
Dale spun the combination, then turned the stainless steel handle. When he opened it, he stood to the side.
"Down on the floor." Tez waved the barrel toward the floor.
"Come on, Tez man. Just take the money, you ain't gotta kill me," pleaded Dale.
"Get the fuck down and shut up."

Dale broke down to his knees and laid on his stomach with his hands stretched out in front of him. His secretary cracked the door and peeked in.
"Dale, I have the Bill of Sale and…" her words fell short at the sight of her boss lying on the floor.
Tez snatched her inside the office and closed the door. "Thank you" he said, taking the keys and paperwork from her.
"Bitch, get down beside him" ordered Tez. He shoved the woman hard in the back, sending her scratching hard against the carpet. Tez stood over Dale with the AR-15 pointed dead at his dome.
"Come on Tez, I have kids man. Just take the money" pleaded Dale.
"Nigga, I know you're not crying. Have some fuckin' dignity."

Tez squeezed off two shots, splattering Dale's brains all over his secretary's face. Her screams were silenced by two dome shots as well. Tez stood up to look at his massacre. It looked like a scene straight out of an episode of *Forensics*. Blood was everywhere, as were their faces. Tez grabbed the ten neat stacks of money from the safe and fanned them at his ear, sounded like about $50,000. 'Not bad' thought Tez. He stuffed the money into his jeans, then packed up his suitcase and grabbed the paperwork to his new Audi A8. Tez locked Dale's office door on his way out and used the front desk phone to call a tow truck. He put the temporary tag in the back window of his Audi and admired the 22" blades as he waited for the tow truck to show up.

A truck from the towing service showed up and Tez told the driver he wanted the 600 SL taken to Platinum Collision over on 7 Mile and Sherwood. He paid him up front, and followed him back to the east side. Abu, the owner of Platinum Collision, was standing out in the

parking lot directing traffic to his workers in Arabic. He turned on his heels and watched the tow truck pull into his shop. Tez jumped out of his car and greeted Abu.
"I got a car for you" Tez smiled.
"What, that old piece of trash?" Abu nodded to the flatbed where the 600 sat.
"What you'll give me?"
"Two grand."
"For a Benz?"
"Take it or leave it" Abu said as he started for the entrance of his shop. Tez wanted to slap the shit out of him and shake him down, but he really needed to off the car. Hehe made a promise to himself that Abu would be somewhere on his list of people to rob.
"A'ight, Abu come on with it" Tez said, catching Abu before he could open the door.
"You know you're getting over," Tez snapped.
"Me? No" Abu said, digging in his pocket. He counted out twenty, one hundred dollars bills into Tez's palm.
"What about that one?" Abu asked about the Audi.
"Maybe in a few months" smiled Tez. He tucked the money deep into his pocket, then climbed back in his new Audi. He peeled out of the lot onto 7 Mile. He took it down to Outer Drive and made a left.

Tez pulled into the parking lot of 007, his once favorite strip club. He hopped out and tossed the keys to the valet. "Handle that may man," he said, falling into the club. Tez took on a D-boy stance under the exit sign awaiting an intro that was not coming. He unfolded his arms and looked around the dimly lit club. His good mood had dwindled just that quickly. He was used to being shouted out as soon as he hit the door by the D.J. They used to shout him out as Nino Brown, but it had been over a year since the last time he'd played 007. The strippers had flipped over along with the D.J.

"You lookin' for somebody?" asked the heavy breathing bouncer to Tez's left.
Tez cracked a smile. "Debo, it's me, Tez."
The man who Tez referred to as Debo looked at him like, "who the hell are you?" "You payin', if not you gotta roll," said Debo.

Tez's smile slowly faded. He dug in his pocket and handed the fat fuck a twenty, then rolled his eyes. He couldn't believe the disdain he was experiencing. That's the streets for you. Tez had been out of commission for too long. When you're getting money, people only smile in your face because you're getting money. Tez got caught up in believing that those people really cared two shits about who he was. He walked over to an empty V.I.P. booth and took a seat. None of the dancers seemed to notice his presence, which infuriated Tez. He knew the remedy for that though. Tez pulled all his money out of his pocket and spread it across the table. If he didn't know anything else, he knew that a bitch was like a blood hound when it came to money, they could smell it. Within seconds, two sleazy strippers slid into Tez's booth at opposite ends, sandwiching him in. They scooted as close as close could get.
"You want a dance, baby?" the one to Tez's right asked, while rubbing herself against him. They were curled up under him like two puppies.
"Nah, I'm cool. But I tell ya'll what you can do for me." Tez said, handing them each $20.
"What's that, baby?" asked the yellow bone to Tez's left. She wrapped her leg around Tez's and waited for him to speak.

"I want both you bitches to raise the fuck up off me, and go douche ya'll pussies. 'Cause one of ya'll is tart as E-mothafucka." The girls looked at Tez in total disbelief and shock. They couldn't believe he had the nerve to come at them like that.

"Beat it" Tez said, shooing them with his hands.
"Probably yo' breath, black ass nigga" the yellow bone said sliding out of the booth.

They stormed inside the dressing room pushing the swinging door open violently. This tickled the shit out of Tez. He had gotten his get back from the way he felt when he first hit the door. His smiled dropped, and his face squinted into a "damn, who you" look, as the finest chick he'd ever seen came walking out of the V.I.P. curtain.
"Slow down, Lil' One" Tez said, quickly sliding around the booth. He stuck his hand out grabbing the girl by the waist, pulling her to him.
"Boy, let go of me."
"I will if you have a drink with me."
"I don't drink" the girl said, looking at all the money sprawled out across the table.
"What do you do?"
"Nothin' like your thinkin'."
What you doin' with all that money on the table like that?"
"I was about to count it. Will you help me, I'll throw you something."
"You just want me to sit with you."
"Can you blame me? Come on." Tez nodded as he scooted back around to the center of the table. "What's your name, Lil' One?" asked Tez.
"Princess, but I like that."
"What?"
"Lil' One."
"Then, that's what it is. They call me, Tez."
"Pleased to meet you" Lil' One said with a smile.
"You gotta forgive me, but baby girl yo' ass is flawless. I'ma have to take another look at you later on."
"You are crazy," laugh Lil' One.
"I'm serious. I ain't never before in my life met a woman half as beautiful as you.

"I think it's just the light."
"No it's not."
"How you get ya' self into strippin'?"
"Bills!"
"I hear you."
"You?"
"What do you mean?" asked Tez.
"I ain't totally new to the streets. Where'd you get all this money from?"
"I'm what they call the ghetto IRS."
"Let me guess, you're robbing people."
"You aren't new to this, are you? You know, we could make a lot of money together."
"How?"
"You ordering something? It's a two drink minimum."

Tez looked up and became furious at the sight of Pharaoh's baby momma Chyna standing over him. Her eyes were glued to her notepad with her pen in hand ready to write. She looked up from her pad and was about to say something slick, but instead she locked eyes with Tez. The night he beat her ass flashed through her mind, him punching her like a man relentlessly.
"Bring me two bottles of Crist." Tez peeled off $700 and told Chyna to keep the change. He watched her intently as she turned on her heels and walked back to the bar.
"You know her?" asked Lil' One.
"Something like that."
"Maybe I should go 'cause I don't need no drama in my life."
"Nah, you good. Ain't nothin' like that. Plus, we 'bout to start getting this money together."
"We'll see."

Chyna came back and set the two bottles on the table. She shot Tez a look of death, then stormed away. Tez wondered if she was still in contact with Pharaoh, but quickly ruled out the possibility. She had shitted on Pharaoh while he was locked up, and the fact that she was still working as a barmaid let Tez know that Pharaoh wasn't fucking with her. He turned back to Lil' One and tried to forget about Chyna.

"So, you fuckin' with me or what?"

"We gone be making money like this, then yeah, I'm fuckin' with you."

"Good" Tez said with a smile. Her removed both bottles from their ice buckets, handing one to Lil' One.

"What are we toasting to?" she asked.

"Blood money." They clinked bottles, then turned them up. Tez had found the missing link to his crazed escapade, Lil' One.

Chapter Six

Ralph rolled onto his back, then reached over to grab Pharaoh's witness list off the night stand. He held it up and dreaded the long list of names to scratch off, but he gave Pharaoh his word. Ralph sat up in bed, still groggy from last night and the night before. He hadn't had a full night's sleep since Pharaoh came home, and he knew that there would be plenty more sleepless nights if he was going to get the list complete. Ralph swung his legs around the side of the bed, stepping into his Air Max. He grabbed his shirt off the night stand and stood up. He pulled his hoody over his head on the way out of his bedroom. Ralph knocked on Swift's bedroom door, which was right across from his. He peeked inside Swift's room and his bed was empty. Ralph stepped inside the bathroom and brushed his teeth and washed his face, then hit the stairs. He could hear the annoying commentator from NBA Live '03 "Scores" and the fast pressing of joystick buttons. Swift and J-Nutty sat side by side in silence playing each other in NBA Live, while Robin and Tuff rolled two morning blunts. Ralph stepped in front of the TV and stopped.

"Fuck you doin', we in the middle of a play-off game" Swift yelled.

"Yeah, nigga move" J-Nutty agreed.

"Pause the game" ordered Ralph. "Pause it before I hit the power button."

"Nigga, what's up?" asked J-Nutty, after pausing the game.

"This is what's up." Ralph unfolded the hit list. "We gotta finish scratching these names."

"Damn, we just hit a head last night" Tuff said.

"Yeah, and when we gone start getting paid?" asked J-Nutty. "Pharaoh's your nigga, not mine."

"Whoa. If it weren't for Pharaoh, my ass would be upstate in Jackson doing a bid, and all ya'll asses would be homeless" Ralph snapped, defending his O.G. – what he was speaking was only the Gospel. It was Pharaoh's house they were all living in and he kept Ralph with enough money for clothes and food. Maybe it wasn't enough to which they expected, but what could they expect?
"Nigga, I make shit happen. If I wasn't staying here, I damn sure wouldn't be homeless" Tuff replied.
"Me neither. I'ma take mines," seconded J-Nutty.
"We doin' all this free head hittin', and for what, to live in this dump?" asked Tuff.
"Swift, how you feel?" asked Ralph.
"I mean you already know I'm ridin' with you, but…"
"There's no life after but, Swift" Ralph said cutting Swift off. "You either ridin' or your not."
"I'm ridin." said Swift.

Ralph looked over at Robin. He was always quiet; all he wanted to do was smoke weed. Ralph knew not to ask Robin because he was gone ride with whatever his brother Tuff wanted to do. So, that left only two Ralph had to convince, J-Nutty and Tuff.
"Look, I already talked to Pharaoh, and he says he's going to bless us something decent once all this shit is over with" Ralph said.
"Something decent like what?" asked Tuff.
"He gone put us on. You know, P ain't no peon. He ain't gone have us on no crumb shit."
"That's all you had to say. Shit, we just wanna know we're not out here on some flunky shit" said J-Nutty.
"I shouldn't have to say that for you to know it. I ain't gone have us on no dummy mission for nobody. Plus, Pharaoh just wants to see where niggas' loyalty lies."
"Who's next on that list?" asked Tuff.

Ralph pulled back a smile. “That’s what I’m talkin’ about. Let’s get this shit done, so we can start gettin’ this money.”

“When?” asked Swift.

“Shit, we can hit this next one right now, then chill for the rest of the day. Go get ready, I’ll be out in the car” Ralph told them. He tucked the hit list in his pocket and hit the front door. Ralph waited in the black Chevy Caprice that Pharaoh had given to him when he first bonded him out of jail. He thought about his promise to handle the business. His loyalty was to Pharaoh first, then his crew. They were being selfish, wanting to be paid at a time like this. Ralph was determined to keep them in line, and if he couldn’t, he’d handle the list himself.

“Damn, my nigga. When you gone get a new car? I’m tired of squeezing up back here” J-Nutty complained, as he, Tuff and Robin all got in the back seat, while Swift rode shotgun.

“Yeah, what happened to the DTS?” asked Tuff.

“You two niggas gone complain all day or what? We gone get our time to shine,” said Ralph.

He turned the key and shifted the car to drive. He pushed the power button on his Kenwood touch screen and Pac’s ‘Shed so Many Tears’ filled the car. Ralph looked in the rear view mirror and just as he suspected, all heads were nodding to the bass line. Pac was their get ready music. 2 Pac would have them young niggas ready to kill something…

Ralph drove deep west, coming up on the John C Lodge Freeway at Hutzel Hospital. He pulled into the parking structure and paid the $2.00 parking fee. The guard working the booth raised the yellow barrier stick and Ralph drove up six ramps to the top level. He pulled on the side of the teal blue Intrepid, and like clockwork J-Nutty slid out of the back seat up to the driver side of the Intrepid. It was like he had keys to the car because within five seconds he was behind the wheel, and another ten seconds he was pulling out of the parking space headed back down the six ramps. The guard who had been sitting inside the booth was now standing in front of the yellow barrier talking into his radio. He tried waving J-Nutty to pull over, but Nutty showed him just why they called him J-Nutty. He gunned the engine, daring the old grey haired black man to stand there. His old ass had enough sense and quickness to move out of the way just in the nick of time. The bumper missed his leg by inches, as J-Nutty crashed through the yellow barrier with Ralph on his heels.

The young hoodlums had learned from their county jail stints after being caught for stealing cars. They learned that it's best to steal a car if it's close to an expressway because the Detroit Police by law can't give chase onto the freeway, only the State Police. This gave them an ample amount of time to disappear from the area and have a better chance of getting away.

Ralph caught up to J-Nutty on the John C Lodge and took the lead. He came up on the Highland Park exit and drove down to Rhode Island Street. He parked in the middle of the block in front of a vacant lot and they all got out, gathering around Ralph.

"Ya'll see that house?" Ralph asked, nodding at a two family flat on the next street over. They were staring at the back of the house through the vacant lot. "That's the nigga Mike's main weed house. Here's his picture." Ralph passed the picture to Swift, who then passed it around.

"He drives a black '96 Impala on black rims. His bitch as should be there or on his way."

"We got him" Swift said.

"Get the nigga done, and get the fuck up outta there. I'ma be waitin' down here on the corner. When ya'll blow past, I'll know ya'll ready and we'll dump the stoly" Ralph explained.

Swift, J-Nutty, Tuff and Robin all piled in the Intrepid and peeled around the corner.

Mike was leaning against the passenger side door of his Impala with his back to the street, totally ignorant to the Intrepid packed to the hilt with killers. Mike had some young hood rat pulled close to him, holding her low at the waist. He was trying to convince the girl to go to the telly with him.

"Come on, I already got us a nice lil' suite downtown at the Double Tree Marriot. We can lay up and order room service after I finish blowing yo' back out."

"You so nasty" laughed the girl.

"I'm so serious. Come on…" pleaded Mike.

"There that bitch nigga go right there. Look, I got this bitch", Swift said, pulling silently on the door handle, leaving his door cracked. Swift crossed the street with his hoody pulled low over his eyes and his 50 cal. Desert Eagle pointed dead at the back of Mike's dome. The girl's smile vanished and her eyes registered with fear. Before Mike could turn around to see what had come over her, Swift knocked his shit loose. His brains splattered all over the girl's face, and his body slumped to the ground. The girl tried screaming, but nothing would come out. She was stuck. Swift walked around the car and gave ole' girl a single dome shot straight through her temple, then put five more in Mike's rat-ass for good measure.

Meanwhile, Tuff and J-Nutty ran up in the weed house. There was no need in leaving empty-handed. A young boy heard the shots and tried to rushed back to lock the door, but Tuff shot straight through the wooden door, killing the boy instantly. J-Nutty caught two of Mike's workers trying to run out the back door, he put four slugs in both of them. He went through their pockets turning up about $800, while Tuff found two pounds of weed in the fireplace. Police sirens could be heard in the distance. "Come on, let's go" Swift said, running inside the house. Tuff grabbed the weed up and searched with his eyes on the way out for anything else of value. Robin sat with the car already in drive. The nosy neighbors were showing up in numbers on their porches, some bold enough to stand on their front lawns. "Oh my God" one older woman said, as Swift, Tuff and J-Nutty all crossed the grass, guns still in hand. They jumped in the whip and Robin burnt out sending a cloud of dust up in the air. They blew past Ralph doing every bit of 80 mph. Robin hit the horn twice, and Ralph peeled away from the curb. Two Wayne County Sheriff's deputies blew past in the opposite direction with their lights flickering and sirens going. Ralph caught up to the Intrepid on Capitol Street. They all climbed in with Ralph, ditching the Intrepid. He burnt back into traffic, and within minutes was riding in the comfort of the Davidson Expressway.

"What took ya'll so long back there?" asked Ralph.

"We had to do some shopping" Tuff explained.

Ralph looked in the back seat at Tuff who was digging in one of the pounds of weed. He shook his head. "We almost got caught for that. What else you get, a few hun'd?"

"Actually $800" J-Nutty said proudly. He broke bread with everybody.

"Look, Ralph. We gone put the work in. But in the mean time until ya' man, Pharaoh puts us on, we still gotta eat," said Tuff.

Ralph was steaming because they just didn't get it. They was on some right now type of shit. The same shit that'll have you doing life in the bing, over nothing. Ralph bit his tongue. 'At least the job got done,' he told himself. He flipped open his cell and texted Pharaoh: '2 down.'

Chapter Seven

It was a late Friday night going into Saturday morning and club 007 was looking like Magic City, packed with balla's from all over the city and the thickets, and the finest strippers in all of Detroit. Tez sat in a V.I.P booth tucked near the rear of the club. He sat alone while he watched the prospects of the night. Cristal, several shots of Remy Martin 1738, and a steak platter filled his table. There were plenty of potential vics playing high-post at the bar and at their V.I.P. booths, but one in particular caught Tez's eye. He zoomed in on the young balla with a mean under stare, and he cut into his steak. Lil' One slid into the booth and wrapped her arms around Tez's neck pulling him in for a kiss on the cheek. She was smiling from ear to ear; Lil' One had fallen for Tez's crazy ass because he's what she was missing missing in her life-- a real nigga.

"Can I get you anything else, baby?" she asked with her arms still draped around his neck.

"Who is that nigga right there?" asked Tez.

Lil' One, discreetly shifted in her seat to face the bar. "Which one?" she asked, of the three men posted at the bar with fists full of money tipping the dancers.

"The nigga who's been sweatin' you all night."

"Ahh, you jealous," teased Lil' One.

"Yeah, of that necklace he got on. I want you to see what's up with the nigga."

"His name is KP, and they say he's gettin' major money. I think he's about twenty."

"Nah, what we talked about. He's gone be our first demo. See if you can't hook it up for the night," Tez said.

"I'ma go see what's up. Is there anything else?"

"Nah, that's it."

Tez watched as Lil' One slid up on KP and his crew. She put the charm on and had KP's young ass wide the fuck open. Lil' One leaned against KP, letting his arms wrap around her waist and slide down, resting on the cuffs of her ass. 'Yeah, work that nigga, bitch,' thought Tez. He sicked Lil' One on KP so that they could rob him. For the past few days, that's all Tez had been doing, was schoolin' Lil' One to the game of setting niggas up. KP was their first project, and judging by all the bling he had on, it was going to be a profitable lick. Tez watched as Lil' One smiled and walked toward the dressing room. From the look on KP's face, Tez could tell that Lil' One had set it up for the night. KP and his crew gave each other dap, and made round motions with their hands to imitate Lil' One's onion booty. Tez took a long swallow from his Cristal, then downed the last two shots of Remy Martin. He stood up and walked over to the bar to pay his tab, nodded at KP and his crew, then exited the club.

"You ready to go?" asked Lil' One, she had changed back into her street clothes, and was standing in front of KP, giving him her undivided attention. KP hit rocks with his men, trying to play big like it was nothing. "I'ma get at ya'll in the A.M." he said. KP looked down at Lil' One from his towering frame. "Nah, question is, are you ready?" Lil' One smiled and didn't bother answering. She pulled the handle up on her suitcase and dragged it out of the club. The valet pulled KP's Suburban XLT to the front; he was sitting on 26's and had more screens than a movie theatre. The sound system made it impossible to hear one another, but provided a vibrant back massage from the roaring sub-woofers tucked in the hatch. Lil' One climbed up into the passenger seat, while KP put her case in the back seat. He didn't turn the music down until getting two blocks away from the club because he had to make a grand exit.

"Where we going?" KP asked, hitting the mute button.

"My apartment" Lil' One replied.

"And where's that at?"

"On Fifteen and Groesbeck."

"That's the 'burbs, how you get out there?"

"The same way you got in this truck, money."

"Who you stay with?"

"I actually stay by myself, why?"

"I'm just asking. Don't need yo' crazy boyfriend, or long, lost lover showing up on no bullshit."

"You ain't gotta worry about that. The only one I'm seeing is the game. Money."

"A'ight…" said KP. He sat back and turned the music up. He was mystified by Lil' One's apartment complex. It wasn't set up like the usual complex; it looked more like high-end condos.

"This where you at?" asked KP, as he pulled into the complex. When'd they build these?"

"About two years ago."

"And how'd you get out here?"

"When they first started advertising the development in the paper, at the time I was lookin' for a place anyway. So, I put down on a unit."

"I might have to get out here. This a nice little duck off." KP parked in one of Lil' One's spaces next to Tez's silver Audi.

Lil' One smiled to herself as she climbed out of the truck. KP grabbed her suitcase and followed her up two flights of stairs to her floor.

"Let me ask you something." Said KP, while Lil' One opened the entrance door.

"What's that?"

"Why all of a sudden you givin' a nigga some rhythm? Before I couldn't get two minutes with you."

"I had to see how hard you'd keep trying, and plus I had to see who you were," Lil' One said as they neared her

apartment door. "And, I don't mess with just no anybody, feel me?"
"I feel you." KP said. He didn't really care either way. He was just geeked that she finally chose him. All that other shit was small talk until the main event.
"Home sweet home" Lil' One said, stepping out of her heels at the door. KP followed suit taking off his Nikes.
"Yeah, I'm feelin' this" he said looking around.

The talk was over. Lil' One went straight to work on KP. She pushed him back against the front door and pulled his shirt over his head and flung it somewhere in the living room. She broke down to her knees unbuckling his pants along the way; she pulled his pants and boxers down around his ankles, the helped him step out of them. KP was left standing there with nothing on, but his jewelry and some white tube socks that came almost up to his ashy knee caps.

Lil' One reached for KP's hard yellow dick and slapped it smooth in her mouth. She deep-throated him, letting the head of his dick brush against the back of her tonsils, then the sides of her jaw. "Hmmm" she moaned, as if it was more pleasurable to her than to him. KP's knees started trembling the head was so good. He had to grip the back of Lil' One's head to keep from falling. His eyes began to water, and with every stroke he could feel the nut rising in the shaft of his dick, ready to explode. Lil' One could sense his readiness and backed off, she wanted to send him out in style. She stood up and walked into the back of the apartment, shedding clothes along the way. KP followed behind her like a lost horny dog, dick leaking and sticking straight out. Lil' One crawled into bed on all fours, then dug her finger deep inside her wet pussy and put it inside KP's mouth to let him taste her juices. She rolled him onto his back and mounted his awaiting dick. "Ohh…" sighed Lil' One on her way down. She buried KP inside her to the hilt. Her clit felt like a wet silk glove giving KP's dick a deep tissue scrub massage, as she slid up and down. Lil' One moved his hands from her hips; she wanted to do all the work. She stopped sliding up and down, and began fucking KP's brains out. She put a pillow over his face to silence his moans and to block the fuck faces he was giving off. Lil' One looked over at the closet which was slightly cracked, and smiled. She could see the whites of Tez's eyes watching. This turned her on more. Lil' One sped up the pace fucking KP's brains out, while looking Tez in the eyes. She could feel the head of KP's dick expanding inside her and knew he was on the brink of busting, so she rolled off him before he could cum inside her. No sooner than she rolled off him, KP started shooting nut everywhere like a volcano erupting. Lil' One reached for his dick and jacked him soft.

"Damn. Shit" KP said, all out of breath. He had worked up a sweat and everything. He was too dazed to sit up. It took him a few seconds to pull his senses together, then he stood up. "Where's the bathroom at?" he asked.

"Right down the hall" Lil' One said, still lying in bed. She watched as KP left the room, then turned her attention to the closet. She smiled, "you enjoy the show?"

"We gone put on a show soon as I get his ass late" whispered Tez.

Lil' One heard the toilet flush, then the door opened. "You say you was paying how much a month?" KP asked, stepping back into the room.

"I didn't say, why? You tryna' pay the rent?"

"I might. If you can keep up that mean little demo you just put down, I just might." KP stopped at the foot of the bed and looked down at his feet. "Why you got all this plastic on the floor?" he asked.

"You ask too many damn questions" said Lil' One.

"Nigga, it's for you" Tez said, stepping out of the closet with his 9 mm Berretta pointed dead on KP.
"How was the pussy?" asked Tez.

KP's mouth dropped to the floor as he stood there on the plastic staring down the barrel of the tiny hole of Tez's silencer. KP swallowed a dry knot caught in this throat, he had the white mouth you get when you know you're about to die.
"Nigga, I asked you a question. How was it?"
"It was alright. I…I guess. Who are…you?" KP stuttered. He was figuring Tez was Lil' One's jealous boyfriend.
"God, nigga." Tez squeezed four silent shots into KP's linky frame. KP buckled over holding his stomach on his way down to the floor, and Tez stood over him putting two more slugs in his dome. He reached down and took KP's Rolex, chain, and bracelet off, putting them on himself.
Tez stood up and looked at himself in the mirror, then back down at KP. "How I look?" he asked, talking to KP.
"You are so crazy…" laughed Lil' One.
Tez turned to face Lil' One. "Baby, how I look? He actin' like a bitch."
"Like a rapper."
"Your hear that? I look betta' than you in your own shit." Tez walked over to one of the recliners beside the bed and stretched out. "Come 'mere. he told Lil' One, who quickly climbed out of bed and into Tez's lap.
"Didn't I tell you we were gone put on a show?" said Tez.
"Yeah, but he's looking at us" Lil' One, said, slightly turning her face up. His eyes were wide open, struck with terror.
"What you lookin' at?" Tez asked, crunching his words together, being sarcastic. "Don't worry about him. Just go start us a shower, and I'ma be in there in a minute. I gotta wrap this bitch up to go" said Tez.

Lil' One stood up and Tez slapped her on the ass as she left the room. Tez rolled KP up into the plastic, then into the thick blanket, wrapping duck tape from top to bottom. Lifting his tall linky ass would be the hard part. Tez found his better half, a ride or die chick in Lil' One. It was gone be a long bloody summer with those two on the prowl.

Chapter Eight

"Oh, baby. Fuck me. Get this pussy" Stacy said in her sexiest light voice. She turned her head back slighty with her eyes closed and the prettiest fuck face on, as Pharaoh long dicked her from the back. "Ahhh," she sighed, as Pharaoh dug deeper with each thrust. He had Stacy's hair wrapped around his hand into a fist, slightly pulling on it just the way she liked it. Sweat trickled down the small of Stacy's back, down between the crack of her ass, mixing in with her juices causing more lubrication for Pharaoh's long black dick, making it even easier to slide in and out. Stacy opened her eyes as she felt herself nearing the point of no return. Her mouth widened as if she was going to scream, but nothing would come out. Her walls started contracting and her vision became a blur. "Oh.." she finally managed, as she slumped her arms over the railing of the balcony. The only thing keeping her up was the death grip of Pharaoh's hands. He released her ponytail and gripped her by her tiny waist, pushing and pulling Stacy from him and back to his satisfaction. "Wait for me" he told Stacy, but she couldn't wait another second. The next stroke sent her into a violent orgasm. Pharaoh caught up and started shooting nut a mile deep inside Stacy. He leaned forward while still stroking her nape.

"I love you Pharaoh." Stacy put her hand on Pharaoh's wet six pack and took a minute to calm down, then pushed Pharaoh out of her. They were both covered in sweat. Their bodies glistened in the morning sun as they stood out on Pharaoh's balcony.

"You get enough?" asked Pharaoh. He was still kissing Stacy. He was charged up and ready to go.

"No. But I think it'll hold me until Friday." Stacy laughed, enjoying Pharaoh's kisses.
Pharaoh stopped for a moment. "Friday?" he asked, then returned to Stacy's breasts.
"Yeah, I do have to work, Pharaoh."
"Baby, you need to get something straight. You don't ever have to work another day in your life unless you want to. We're straight."
"Pharaoh, I can't just quit my job. What am I 'pose to do then?"
"Be with me. We'll be together." Stacy didn't say anything. She took a deep breath, then sighed. She let her eyes drift off across the Detroit River.
"What's wrong, baby?" asked Pharaoh, as he caressed Stacy's head.
"I have less than ten years before I retire, I'm not leaving the force, Pharaoh. Besides, I'm a grown ass woman."
"What do you mean by that?"
"I can't just up and leave what I'm doing, my life. Pharaoh, right now you're on the run, and if they…"
"Nah, don't stop. Finish what you were going to say."
""'Just forget it."
"Oh, I get it. You don't think I'ma come from under this shit, huh?"
"I didn't say that."
"But that's what you meant. I mean let's be real with each other. You don't think I'll ever be able to live a normal life again, do you?"
"That's the thing. I don't know. Pharaoh, I want to live a normal life. I'm 41, I ain't got time to be living a life on the run."
Pharaoh grabbed Stacy by her waist pulling her to him. "Look at me" he ordered. He didn't speak until their met eyes. "How long have you been holding that in
"A minute."

"Answer me this. Do you think what I'm doing is far-fetched, or unlikely to happen?"

Stacy's eyes welled up, she wiped a lone tear from the corner of her eye before it could stream down her pretty face. "That's what I'm afraid of. Pharaoh, I don't know what's going to happen. I love you too, but maybe we should just enjoy the time we have together and see what happens." She tried to kiss Pharaoh's lips, but he turned away. "I gotta get ready for work" she said, trying to look into Pharaoh's eyes. She walked around him over to the outdoor shower.

Pharaoh put his shorts on and leaned over the railing staring off into Detroit. He had no idea Stacy was feeling like that, and at the moment he didn't know what to feel. Part of him wanted to say fuck Stacy and just do him, but his loyal side was getting the best of him. Pharaoh felt like he owed Stacy his life for helping him escape. Without her, none of his other plans would even be possible. But why? Why didn't she believe in him? Pharaoh squinted at the sky-line of Detroit, with rage and fury in his eyes. "This is all your fault. Everything" Pharaoh said, talking to Tez. "You fucked my life up." Pharaoh was so angry that he wanted to cry, but he knew crying never fixed anything. The only thing that could solve Pharaoh's problems was blood, Tez's blood. Pharaoh turned around to lean against the rail. He watched as Stacy finished showering and drying off. She walked over to him leaving a trail of wet footprints on the concrete along the way. "Let me." Pharaoh took the towel from Stacy. He turned her around and blotted her back and arms dry. He turned her around quickly, snatching her into his arms. He slicked her wet hair back while staring down into her eyes.

"Maybe you're right. We should just enjoy our time together and see what happens. But I'll always love you," said Pharaoh. His love was much more out of loyalty.

"I love you too."
"So, Friday we have a date?"
Stacy smiled. "It's a date." Stacy gave Pharaoh a long kiss. She had to pull herself away because if she kissed him a moment longer, she'd end up having to take another shower. "Friday" she said, letting her nails travel down Pharaoh's stomach as she walked around him toward the house.

Pharaoh stretched out on one of the deck chairs and grabbed his binoculars from beside him. He fretted over not being able to return to Detroit. He watched the cars travel across the Ambassador Bridge, some going while others coming. Pharaoh sat the binoculars down. He couldn't stand to watch anymore, he was only torturing himself. He closed his eyes and tried to think about something other than killing Tez.
"What up doe, old head?" said Ralph, taking a seat next to Pharaoh.
"A…what it is? Give me some news I can use," said Pharaoh.
"Two down. You get my texts?" asked Ralph.
"Yeah, I got 'em but who you hit?"
"That nigga Chris and Mike."
"Okay, any word on Tez?"
"Not yet. I went past his crib a few times, but it looks empty. But two white boys in a Lumina be parked out there."
"We can't let that stop us. Shit, they can get it too," said Pharaoh, sitting up.
"I ain't stuntin' them. I'm just waiting to see if the nigga show his face first."
"Yeah, you don't want to miss."
"Exactly…"
"But what up doe. You came to check on your old head or what?" Pharaoh asked, smiling.

"Yeah, came to check you out. Who was baby girl I saw on the way out?"
"Oh, that's my piece, Stacy."
"Yeah, she's definitely a piece. You ain't holla at them white hoes no more?"
"Nah, but I'ma need to. Shit, I ain't been doing nothing except sitting out here watching the boats pass by."
"So, that's what you do when you're old and rich, sit out here and watch boats, huh?"
"After a while it gets boring. I'm ready to get back to the city."
"You ain't missing nothin' my nigga."
"Don't tell me that. I hate it when people tell me that shit. I'm missing life right now."
"I got you P. I'ma get it done, just give me some time."
"I know you're going to take care of business. I'm just venting right now. That bitch nigga fucked my life up, Ralph. The shit fuckin' with me so bad that all I can think about is killin' him. I see that nigga's face when I close my eyes and when I wake up. I use to love Tez like a brother, that's what hurts."

Ralph didn't try to interject, he just listened. He figured that's what Pharaoh needed at the time, for someone to just listen while he let it all out. "We gotta get his ass," Pharaoh said, turning to face Ralph. He had tears in his eyes, so Ralph turned his head out of respect. Ralph had never seen Pharaoh like this before. He was always the strong one, the one who always kept everything together. It was the seeds of doubt Stacy had planted about his plan maybe not being realistic. Pharaoh was starting to second guess himself, which is something he never does. 'I gotta get Tez and Stacy outta my mind, so I can start thinking clear' thought Pharaoh. He was careful not to drop a tear. He just held his head back and let the welling tears dry into his sockets.

Ralph came to see Pharaoh for two reasons, to check on him and to express the concerns of his crew wanting to be paid. But now wasn't a good time to bring that up. Pharaoh needed to know someone had his back and not just on the strength of what he could do for them. If Ralph had to, he'd handle the list by his lonely, or die tryin'. He had nothing but love and respect for Pharaoh, and he would put it all on the line for him on any given day. Ralph put his arm around Pharaoh and promised him that he'd clean things up.

"How's your little knuckle head crew?" asked Pharaoh.

"They straight," Ralph lied

"Tell 'em I more than appreciate it, and that it won't be forgotten." It wasn't details, but it was a promise coming from Pharaoh, and his word was platinum.

Ralph nodded. He already knew Pharaoh was gone bless them, he shouldn't have to say it because of knowing his character, just how he looks out on G.P. – they all should have known he'd look out in the end. "That's what I told 'em" Ralph said, feeling even more assured.

Chapter Nine

"What can I get for you Willie G?" asked Killer B, he stood behind the counter of Sammy's Blue Note serving soul food and desserts.
"Give me some rib tips and a side of greens and macaroni & cheese" ole Wille G said. He was a regular at the hole-in-the wall juke joint.

Sammy's Blue Note was a jazz bar where old heads would come to enjoy the live sets provided by local talent and some washed up musicians still holding on to a dream of making it. The crowd was no younger than fifty, and everybody knew everybody. Tonight was open mic Wednesday, the stage was open to all, so there was a nice turn out like any other Wednesday. After the open mic session, the old heads would grab a partner and juke out on the dance floor. Good ole' fun, they called it. Killer B's real name is Brian. He had taken the job as manager, cook, server, and janitor. He basically manned the hole-in-the-wall by himself for a measly $400 per week, which old man Sammy paid him under the table. Brian was Pharaoh's uncle, one of the main snitches on his case. After losing his street-cred, Brian stopped hustling altogether and got on some family man shit like most rats do. After giving Pharaoh up to the feds, all he wanted to do was work and take care of his family. But, the past will never forget, and Pharaoh's motto was 'God might forgive you, but I won't!'

Brian had been working at Sammy's for over a year now. Even though the money wasn't all that, he had grown to be content. He served all the old heads their rib tips and sides with the cheesecake and other deserts. It was nearing 11:00 p.m. and the old heads were filing out of the joint on their way home. The fun was good, but their old bones were tired and ready to lay it down. "You take it easy Mae" said Brian, handing the woman he called Mae her food over the counter. Mae was the last customer. Brian walked her to the front door and locked it, then stepped back into the eatery. He looked at the clock on the wall; it was now 11:15. He figured he could be home by 11:45 eating left over rib tips with his wife while curled up in bed. His rat ass had no remorse for telling on Pharaoh and ruining his life, and he was supposed to be his uncle. He'd go home every night to his family, while keeping Pharaoh from his. Brian had devised a work plan, so that when the club closed he could rush through the clean up. He already had his mop water ready, sinks full of soap-sudded water for the pans and his rags for the tables. He knocked everything out in fifteen minutes. He packed up enough leftovers for his family into Styrofoam trays. He grabbed his coat, killed the lights and was out the door. Brian set the plastic bag down while he locked up. He'd been hanging around those old heads so much that he started dressing like them. He had on some slacks, a spring coat, loafers, church socks, and a bop hat.

Ralph almost didn't recognize the nigga, as he got in the car. Brian set the leftovers in the passenger seat of his '85 Grand Prix that had seen better days. He stuck the key in the ignition and started the car. He flicked through the presets on his ancient tape deck, then pulled the neck shift down to reverse. He backed out of his lone parking space and turned his headlights on. The lights from his car provided the only source of light on pitch black Grover St. where the Eastern Market sat. Brian hummed the words to 'The Isley Brothers' "For the love of you…I know that I'm living…" He reached over and opened one of the trays. He began feeding his face with rib tips while cruising down Grover St. He stopped at the corner of Cherrylawn, briefly pausing, then made a slow right while still stuffing his face

and humming to the Isley Brothers. The car wobbled and the frame squeaked as Brian crossed a set of railroad tracks. That was Ralph's cue to let him know they were now on Leslie Street, which was another pitch black street, and a dead end, literally for Killer B. Ralph popped up like a jack in the box. His narrow frame made it easy for him to crunch down in the back seat of Brian's two door Grand Prix. Ralph put the cold steel barrel to the back of Brian's dome and cocked the hammer back.
"Don't shoot me man, please" Brian pleaded. His eyes bucked with fear, as he looked through the rear-view mirror.
"Pull over" ordered Ralph. "And cut the lights off."
"I'll give you the money, just please don't kill me."
"Shut the fuck up and pull over."
"Okay," Brian said, dropping his barbeque rib tip so that he could grip the wheel with both hands. He turned the wheel slightly and killed his lights, all the while looking at Ralph through the mirror. Ralph looked over at the houses for a second, and all Brian needed was that split second. He grabbed the door handle and jumped out of the car while it was still rolling toward the curb.
"Shit!" yelled Ralph. He had let the nigga jump out.

The car hit the curb, then rolled back. Ralph struggled to push the seat up, but finally got out of the car. He took aim as he stood in the middle of the street at Brian's back. He was bookin' down the dark street hollering, "Help me!..." Ralph lowered his gun and began after him on foot. There was no way Brian was going to out run Ralph. His old ass was out of shape and some more shit. The only thing keeping him up and running was fear, but fear alone wouldn't save him from the retribution hawking him down.
"Somebody call the police! Help!..." Brian said, but to no avail. None of the lights to the houses came on, and no one came outside. It was his time to go.
"Oh, shit. Look at this nigga," J-Nutty pointed.

"What the fuck. That's crazy" laughed Swift. They were parked two blocks down from the tracks facing the opposite direction; they were to wait there for Ralph after he murked ole' Killer B. They held their sides in laughter.
"Oh, shit. This a wild nigga" J-Nutty said. He turned on his high beams nearly blinding Killer B. He and Swift got out of the car, while Killer B came to a screeching stop. He looked back at Ralph who was gaining on him, then at the two shadows standing in the headlights.
Killer B made one last effort to gain someone's attention. "Help!" he screamed deep from the pits of his soul. His face registered with death, as J-Nutty and Swift pulled their guns from their waist.
"Please, just take the money" pleaded Killer B, while back stepping. He backed dead into Ralph's barrel.
"Get yo' bitch ass down!" ordered Ralph. He slapped Killer B across the head sending him to the ground. "Got me chasing yo' bitch ass all around" Ralph said, breathing hard as ever. Swift and J-Nutty stood over him with their guns pointed down at his dome.
"Hold up, let me get a picture of his hoe ass" Ralph said. He pointed his camera phone down at Killer B and said "smile for the camera, bitch."
"Why are ya'll doing this?" asked Killer B. He was nursing the gash on the back of his head.
"I got a message from Pharaoh" said Ralph, after snapping a picture.

Killer B's eyes damn near popped out of his head at the sound of Pharaoh's name. Ralph raised his gun and together, he, J-Nutty and Swift filled Killer B's frame with hot balls. His body jerked violently as he welcomed the slugs. Swift gave him two dome shots, knocking a patch of flesh out the side of his face. It was overkill the way they slaughtered him. Just the type of death his rat-ass deserved to die--a bitch ass death. Ralph snapped another picture, then sent them both to Pharaoh, one to show the fear in his eycs before he received his retribution, and the other to show the consequences of snitching. Ralph then sent Pharaoh a text: "3 down! I told yo' old ass to fall back and let the youngin' handle B.I. I got you my nigga." Ralph wanted to speed the list up to show his O.G. that business was being handled and that he wasn't sitting on his hands. Ralph was busting his gun and he needed Pharaoh to know it! So, he sent Robin and Tuff to hit another head, while he hit Killer B's head. He figured if they worked it like that, they'd have the list knocked out in half the time.

Chapter Ten

The back room of Al's Barbershop was packed to the hilt with old sweaty millionaires and a few thousandaire -type niggas. All the major playas, hustlas, and pushas stood gathered around the makeshift casino style crap table lobbying for bets. It was Wednesday night getting ready to go into Thursday morning, and not one of the men had to worry about getting up for work in the morning. Hustling and gambling was their work, had been all their lives. In the back of Al's, time wasn't a factor, it didn't exist. No one cared what time it was because they were where they wanted to be, packed in the back room of Al's trying to beat each other out of some serious cold, hard cash. Tonight they were having a $100,000 lock-out, everyone had to have at least $100,000 to get in.

The bets started at $1,000 and went up a grand every hour. They were now betting $5,000 in the center. "He needs a fader in the center," Pete instructed. Maurice stood at the corner of the table leaned over, shaking the large clear and white dice under his hand. He was waiting for Teacher to finish counting out the money. "Take off, Mo" Pete said. He was the house man cutting the game on behalf of Maurice. Maurice tossed the dice across the line up against the back wall. They landed on eleven. "He still needs a fader" Pete repeated, scraping the money toward Maurice, leaving enough in the center to cover the fade. Mo' was hot tonight. He always seemed to come out on top along with the other three members of the Love Brothers, Rich Bo, Redman and Old Man Bob. They always bet together, and always won because they figured out of the four, at least one would catch the hot hand, while the rest rode him like a horse betting on him. "Let 'em ride" said

Teacher, getting his $5,000 to the center. Mo' took off and stuck another natural. "Seven. The man still needs a fader, not a friend" Pete laughed, scooting Mo' his winnings.

Ole' shiesty ass Dee picked up on the Love Brothers' tactic, and rode Mo' like a horse too. He had to play the back drop because for real he wasn't even supposed to be in their game. Dee's money wasn't long enough to be involved in no $100,000 lock-out. Hell, he didn't have $20,000 to his name. Since Pharaoh took his fall, the weed money Dee was used to getting ceased to exist. So, he did what he did best, try and crawl up a nigga's leg. Dee swallowed bets, picking and choosing what he'd bet on. Basically he was looking for sucka bets, and he found one. The young North end cat, Blaze, didn't know that Dee only had two grand and some change on him. He'd let Dee sucker him into about four dumb ass bets, until Blaze raised the question. "The way you bettin', you sure you got a hun'd stacks on you?" All eyes turned to Dee. That was a good ass question? He had swallowed bets all night and in the past. All the other playas wanted to know if he was taking shots at their money. The discussion caused Mo' to lose his momentum, he crapped out in two rolls. He looked at Dee with a look that said, "get the hell outta here, now!" Dee got the message loud and clear. Mo' was Al's youngest son, he ran the shop and hosted all the crap games. His face was on the game. So, when he put the stipulation out there that it was a lock-out, that's what the gamblers were expected to shoot at, nothing less. Mo' apologized to all the men for Dee swallowing bets and assured he would never set foot in their game again! Dee didn't care for real. He sat in his barber chair, kicked his feet up, and counted his winnings for the night. He had close to $8,000. His petty ass counted it a second, then a third time with a smile on his face. "Not bad," he said folding the money and stuffing it into his pocket. He patted it for safe keeping, then reclined in his chair. Dee looked at the clock on the wall, it was going on three o'clock and the game showed no signs of slowing down. He couldn't leave yet because he was supposed to be working the door and watching people out to their car as they left. Dee closed his eyes figuring he could steal a few hours of sleep, then maybe he'd get to go home for a shower, and come back to open up the shop for the morning customers. Within minutes he was snoring and out like a light.

Four hours later the game finally broke up, with Maurice and the Love Brothers reigning champs. They hit the game for over a million. They'd meet up at Rich Bo's crib and break bread later to equal out everyone's portion. It wasn't that they were hustling the game or cheating, they just played the odds, and the odds were slim to none on the chance they'd all lose for the night. Four sharp shooters, how could they miss? If one was off for the night, somebody would step up and catch fire. Tonight it was the youngest of the bunch, Mo'. Mo' walked up to Dee's chair and tapped his leg. "Dee, come let us out" said Maurice. Dee strained to open his eyes. He grunted as he sat up and stood to his feet. He just knew Mo' was about to chew his ass for the episode earlier. But Mo' hadn't said anything about it. He was too busy cheesin' and talking shit with his cohorts. 'Yeah, they must've won again. Good,' thought Dee, as he opened the door. Now he wouldn't have to hear Mo's bitchy mouth about how he janked the whole game, and all the other superstition shit Mo' strongly believed in. "We gone start callin' you Crawl," said Rich Bo. He was joking at Dee. "Crawl, 'cause you always tryin' to crawl up a nigga's leg." They all shared a laugh. Dee knew to laugh, or at least fake a smile. They were millionaires, thus making any and everything they said funny.

"I'ma catch ya'll later," Mo' told his cohorts from the entrance. He and Dee stood in the door.

"Aren't you going to go home and get some rest?" he asked Dee.
"For what, one hour? The shop's about to open up. I'ma change and wash up here, I caught a few hours of sleep."
"Well, I'll see you in the afternoon" Mo' daid.
Dee locked the door up then stepped inside the bathroom to take a bird bath.

*****

"What you think he got in the case?" Tuff asked Robin. He was watching Mo' as he power walked toward the parking lot with a black case at his side.
"Either clippers or money" Robin replied.
"I bet it's some money. Them old niggas wasn't in their all that time cutting no hair."
"I heard they be shootin' dice in the back room, all the major figures be in there."
Tuff watched Mo' like a lion on its prey. "You thinkin' what I'm thinkin'?" asked Tuff.
"Yeah, but we gotta get ole' boy's rat-ass. We can't blow our chance."

Mo' tossed the case in the back seat of his sapphire 420 Benz, then he climbed behind the wheel. "There goes God knows how much money" Tuff grumbled as he watched Mo' skirt out of the parking lot down 7 Mile Rd. slowly fading into the distance. All he could see after a while was the white tail pipe smoke from the cool morning air.
"Fuck it, I'ma take it out on rat-ass" Tuff said.
"Where the fuck is he at?"
"I don't know, but that's his beat up ass Seville sittin' right there." Tuff nodded to Dee's black Caddy parked at the curb.
"What time do they open up? He's probably still in there?"
"I think 'bout eight maybe" Tuff answered as his met eyes with the driver of a passing Detroit Police car. "These

bitches betta not turn around" he said, now watching the two white officers through his side mirror.

They should have thanked God that they didn't turn around because Tuff had a fully automatic SKS sitting between his legs. Airing their white asses out would have looked excellent on his ghetto resume. Tuff and Robin were parked across the street in front of BB's Diner in a stolen Astro van, sipping Henny and chain smoking the weed they took from Mike's weed house. "By the time we finish blowing this L, the shop should be getting ready to open" Robin said, as he flicked the flame of his lighter at the tip of the blunt. He twirled the blunt around the flame to make sure it was evenly lit, then put it in his mouth. The fire turned burnt orange as he pulled on the blunt hard. Robin hit the L twice, then passed it to Tuff. It was just another blood mission for the two young head hitters. There wasn't much of a plan, just go in and kill the nigga, and take whatever money he had on him. To them, killing somebody was the easiest thing in the world. All they had to do was squeeze the trigger and watch the body fall to the floor. They had long ago lost any sense of emotion or compassion for anyone else outside of them and their crew. Growing up on the streets with no one they could turn to or count on made their young hearts as cold as ice, and they wouldn't hesitate to let someone else share in their pain.

"Nah, I'm good. Go head and kill it." Tuff said, waving the blunt off. He clutched the stock of his SKS, while he waited for Robin to finish the blunt.

"You ready?" asked Robin, as he flicked the roach out the window.

Tuff tucked the short SKS into his pants the best that he could and pulled his hoody over the stock. "Let's go" he said, pulling on the door handle. He waited for Robin to walk around the front of the van; they waited for two cars to pass, then crossed the street. Robin pushed the doorbell, while Tuff stood with his back against the wall. Dee had finished taking his bird bath and he had laid back in his chair and drifted back off to sleep. "Damn it" he said agitated, as he opened his eyes at the sound of the buzzer. The sleep was just starting to get good. He got up and squinted at the surveillance monitor mounted on the wall. Seeing a young boy, Dee buzzed him in. He walked around the back of his barber chair and clicked on his sanitizer box and grabbed his cape.

"Ya'll know we don't open until eight, for future reference" Dee said, now facing Tuff and Robin. "Who's first?" he asked.

Robin looked at Tuff and shrugged. "I'm good, you go head" Tuff said. Robin took a seat in one of the waiting chairs. He figured they'd send Dee out in style, let him cut his last head, then they'd hit his head.

"How you want it?" Dee asked, wrapping the cape around Robin.

"Low tapered, two with the grain" answered Robin.

Dee ran a comb through Robin's scalp, then clicked on his clippers. "You can turn the TV on, young blood" Dee said, tossing Tuff the remote. "Put it on the news." He began blending the back of Robin's neck, working his barber comb like butter, making a perfect blend, all while watching the news. "Turn that up, young blood." Dee stopped cutting Robin's hair and focused on the "breaking news" story. His eyes narrowed, then grew wide at the sight of Killer B's mugshot. He remembered him from the day at the county jail and federal building. He was on Pharaoh's case, as was he. The camera man zoomed in on the blood stained concrete, while the reporter explained that was where police found the victim Brian Dickson shot to death.

"That's fucked up" said Dee.

Tuff turned to Dee. "Why? That nigga's a rat."

"How you know that?" asked Dee.

"That's what the bottom of the screen said, it said he was an informant."
"That's still fucked up, killed that man like that in cold-blood." Dee was putting a line on Robin's head. His face was screwed up thanking his lucky stars that it wasn't him.
"That's the game. You gotta expect that when you play the game and break the rules" Tuff said.
"What are the rules, 'cause I damn sure don't remember ever seeing them in writing," Dee snapped. He stopped for a moment awaiting Tuff's answer.
"No snitching. That's the first and only rule. Everything else as playas of the game we gotta charge it to the game."
"You've been watchin' too many damn mafia movies, and fillin' your head with all that rap garbage. Ain't but one rule in the game, and it's called save yo' self" said Dee. He was finished with Robin's shape-up, and was dusting the loose hairs from his face.
"That's why the cemetery is filled with rat-ass niggas just like you for having that same rat-ass mentality," Tuff said, standing up.
"Whoa young blood, where all that comin' from? We just kickin' the game around" Dee replied. He pulled the cape off Robin and snapped it a few times. "Fifteen dollars" Dee said.
"I'll pay 'em" said Tuff. He lifted up his hoody and pulled the SKS out. Dee damn near shitted on himself as Tuff raised the black beast to his chest. "Yo' rat-ass been out here skating for too long. Somebody shoulda' killed you long time ago."
"What's up, young blood?" Dee asked, stomach sitting close to his ass. He was so scared his soul was ready to take off running and leave him standing there.
"Figure it out on your way to hell" Tuff said, squeezing back on the trigger, 223 shells riddled Dee's short pudgy frame.

Chunks of flesh and blood splattered against the back mirror and barber chair. Dee tried to keep his feet under him, but the blast was too powerful as Tuff laid on the trigger until Dee crashed down on the floor. He stood over Dee and looked down at him. Dee was choking and gagging on his own blood. "I would put you outta your misery, but you need to suffer" Tuff said. Robin was already rummaging through Dee's pockets, lifting the $8,000. "Jack pot."

"Come on, let's get the hell out of here" Tuff said. They left him to choke on his own blood and bleed to death. Four down.

Chapter Eleven

"Who's the red nigga sittin' in front of the stage? Tez asked, Lil' One.
"That's Yacht" said Lil' One. They were watching the Friday night ballers from afar in Tez's V.I.P. booth.
"Is that right?" said Tez. He had his murda mask – ice grill on. In his mind, there was no way in hell all them niggas was supposed to be stuntin' as hard as they were, especially this high yellow nigga named Yacht. He looked pussy. All Tez could think about was, 'ain't nobody robbed him yet?'
"What's that BBC shit stand for on his shirt?"
"Billionaire Boys Club."
"What kinda goofy shit is that, where these niggas from, Nebraska?"
"No. They from the West side of Detroit. BBC is some shit Yacht started, saying that you had to be gettin' fifty bricks or better to become a member."
"So, all them niggas standing around him, they all gettin' fifty bricks?"
"At least" Lil' One replied. "They 'bouts to get ready to call me for my set."
"See what's up, if you can't hook it up for tonight."
"You sure we want to fuck with Yacht? He ain't no regular nigga..." Lil' One said, sliding out of the booth.
"Fuck him and them pussy ass niggas standing around him. They all regular niggas when that trumpet staring 'em in the face. They go to cryin' like bitches" Tez growled. He had become furious that Lil' One would even ask him some stupid shit like, "is he sure?" Tez got a thrill out of watching tough niggas bitch up.
"Okay, just calm down, Tez. I will try to hook it up" said Lil' One. She leaned over and gave Tez a kiss on his cheek,

then softly ran her hand down his face, as if to calm him down.

Tez watched as Lil' One seductively climbed the stairs to the stage. Everything in the club started moving in slow motion, conversations stopped in mid-sentence, and every eye focused on the thickness of Lil' Ones thighs. As she reached the stage the D.J. put her theme song on, Freeway's 'What We Do is Wrong'. Niggas went crazy as the song dropped and Lil' One rode the beat like Jay-Z did on the track. All the ballas gathered around the stage showering Lil' One with hundreds and fifties. When she finished her set, she scraped up every bit of $3,000. She folded the money into her garter belt, then exited the stage.

"You know it's more where that came from" Yacht said, reaching for Lil' One's hand as she passed.

"And who are you?" asked Lil' One.

"Like I need an introduction. Quit playin', you know who I am. Question is, you tryna' go home with a boss tonight and make this twenty stacks?"

"Twenty stacks, to do what?" asked Lil' One.

"What you think. To fuck or get lost," Yacht laughed. He was an ignorant mothafucka, as arrogant as they came.

"I don't know, you too bold for me" said Lil' One.

"Nah, it's called real nigga shit. I'm too rich to be lying and playin' cat & mouse games. It is what it is. Either you is or you ain't. Really it's nothin'." Yacht turned, giving Lil' One his back, as he went back to kicking it with Fat Mike and Jessie James of the Street Lordz.

"She still standing there?" asked Yacht.

"Nah, she went in the dressing room" Jessie James replied.

"That's how you boss up on a bitch. You cut that hoe down, then spinned on her" said Fat Mike, as he downed his last shot of Patron.

"Nah, I wasn't even gone stunt on the bitch until she tried to stunt on me, actin' like she don't know who a nigga is. Like we peons or something."
"There she go now. She comin' this way" Jessie said.

Yacht played it cool, tossing back a double shot of Grey Goose, then chasing it with a swallow of Moet. Lil' One stopped dead in front of Yacht and shifted all her weight onto one leg and folded her arms. Yacht lowered the bottle of Moet and stared at Lil' One for a few seconds before saying anything.
"What, you changed your mind?"
"Something like that" said Lil' One.
"I knew you would. Twenty G's always does."
"Where are you going to take me?"
"To the Netherland Ranch, why? Does it matter?"
"Nah, I'm just asking…" said Lil' One.
Yacht turned up his bottle taking a long swallow, then slammed it empty down on the bar.
"I'ma get up with you boys tomorrow. I'ma go blow baby girl's back out" Yacht said to Fat Mike and Jessie James. He was carrying on like Lil' One wasn't even standing there. He gave them a pound and slapped them on the shoulder before turning to face Lil' One. With his eyes glossy from the liquor and champagne, Yacht looked down at Lil' One.
"You ready to go?"
"Yeah." Lil' One smiled at Fat Mike and Jessiee James, as Yacht led the way out of the club.

Lil' One winked at Tez who was sitting out in the parking lot ducked low in his seat watching the front door. The valet pulled Yacht's burgundy Bentley up to the door and held the door open for Yacht. Lil' One climbed in the passenger seat and flipped down the mirror inside the visor to check her pretty. When she pushed the visor up, Yacht was already unbuckling his belt and unbuttoning his pants.

Lil' One looked at him like he was crazy, as he pulled his limp dick through his boxer shorts.
"You are bold as hell with yo' shit" Lil' One said with an attitude.
"Nah, I keep tellin' you I'm real with mine. Ain't no need of playin' with it. You know what it is" said Yacht, as he leaned his seat back a little. "Come 'mere" he said, reaching for the back of Lil' One's head. She didn't try to refuse him.

Tez saw Lil' One's head go down into Yacht's lap, as he followed them from about five cars behind. "That's right, baby. Put that platinum head on him" Tez said, as he fired up a blunt. He didn't care if she sucked a thousand niggas' dicks, as long as they were sitting on some cheese it was all good.

Yacht was a boss in every sense of the word, a made man on the streets of Detroit and other major cities. What Yacht wanted, Yacht got. Lil' One wasn't the first stripper he paid $20,000 for one night with him, and she wouldn't be the last in his mind. She was just the latest chick- Ms. New Booty. Next week he'd be driving the same route home, but with a different set of lips wrapped around his dick. See, Yacht had rules when it came to a chick riding in his cars. He and his click deemed it illegal for a chick to get in their car and not suck their dick. They'd tell a bitch in a minute, "occupy ya'self" and then pull out their dick. It was also a way to keep the chicks from knowing where their going, 'cause a lot of chicks try to read signs, so they can either set a nigga up or pop up unannounced. Lil' One "occupied" herself for the entire 45 minute drive out into Bloomfield, Michigan where Yacht's $10,000,000 mansion was located.
"That's enough, save some for when we get inside," said Yacht, as he pulled into his driveway. He pushed the garage door button clamped to the visor, then pulled in.

Tez parked two properties down. He killed his lights before turning onto Yacht's street, so he missed him. The platinum head on Lil' One's shoulders was known to do that. Tez eased his door closed, then crossed the street blending into the darkness. He rolled under the garage door just before it shut and laid on the passenger side of the car. Lil' One damn near screamed when she got out of the car and saw Tez put his finger to his mouth and waited for Yacht to get out of the car. He was still pulling up his pants. As soon as Yacht got out and closed the door, Tez popped up looking like the Angel of Death dressed in all black. Yacht dropped his keys and back stepped toward the wall. Tez matched his steps until cornering Yacht against the back wall. Yacht's face turned pale white, as he stared down the barrel of the black 40 cal. pointed dead at his face. "You set me up, bitch" Yacht yelled.

"You hear that, baby?" Yacht here is a genius" Tez laughed. He opened his free arm and pulled Lil' One close to him, giving her a kiss. Lil' One leaned against Tez's strong frame, while looking Yacht in the eyes.

"I'ma ask you one time, not twice, but once. Where that shit at?" asked Tez.

"What shit?" asked Yacht.

*Boom!...*Tez lowered his gun to Yacht's knee cap and shot him.

"Fuck!" yelled Yacht, clutching his knee. His jeans were starting to stain with dark blood, and the blood was seeping through the jeans onto his hands.

"Consider that your warning shot" Tez said. He stood over Yacht and pressed the barrel deep into his temple. "The next one, you won't remember.".

"Okay, it's upstairs in my closet underneath a shoe rack," Yacht shot off, sounding like an infomercial.

Tez nodded to Lil' One to go check it out. "A'ight. Now get your bitch-ass on your feet and open this door" Tez demanded, standing next to the entry door leading into the house.

Yacht dragged himself over to the door and opened it. Lil' One went to check out the stash spot.

"Get yo' ass in there. Don't nobody feel sorry for you just cause yo' knee fucked up" Tez yelled. He slapped Yacht across the head with his gun 'cause he wasn't moving fast enough. Blood skeeted against the wall and in the air. Yacht grabbed the back of his head and yelled like a whore on his way to the floor. "You betta hope that shit is up there." Tez reached down, grabbing Yacht up by his shirt. He pushed him through the house into the spacious living room. Tez shoved him onto one of the snow white sofas and held him at bay, while Lil' One rummaged for the work.

"You think you're going to get away with this?" asked Yacht.

"You still talkin' shit?" asked Tez.

"I already know you're gone kill me, so fuck you. But you won't get away with it."

This infuriated Tez. The fact that Yacht was talking shit, he was supposed to be begging for his life. "Bitch-nigga, you know you're scared straight, so stop faking."

"Nigga, fuck you!" yelled Yacht. "I'm a made man. Fuck you!"

Tez couldn't stand it anymore. He wanted to make sure Lil' One had gotten the work, but he blanked out. *Boom! Boom! Boom!* He hit Yacht three times in the dome, center mask. He kept squeezing shots into Yacht's chest until the clip was empty. "Talk shit now! Talk yo' shit now, bitch nigga!" yelled Tez.

"Baby, what are you doing?" asked Lil' One. She pulled Tez's arm trying to break his trance.

"You get everything?" asked Tez.

"Yeah. He was short though. There was only twenty bricks."

"What about money?"
"Some, but we gotta count it. Come on, let's get out of here" Lil' One said, looking at Yacht's bloody body.
"You owe me thirty bricks, bitch nigga. Have my money when I get back" Tez said sarcastically.
"You are so crazy," laughed Lil' One. She handed Tez the duffle bag, and pulled on his arm.
"Let's go, baby," she said, dragging him out of the house. Tez wanted to rummage around the crib for more money and jewelry, but Lil' One wouldn't let him. They were officially the 30' Bonnie & Clyde.

Chapter Twelve

Pharaoh was spending a lot of time at Déjà vu Strip Club right outside of Windsor, Canada. Besides watching boats inch down the Detroit River all day, there wasn't much else to do, but go look at some ass and pretty titties. The girls loved Pharaoh because of his accent, and the fact that he was an American. He was treated like royalty from the time he set foot in the club until the time he left. All the strippers dreamed of marrying an American man, so they could go over to the United States. Pharaoh told them all his name was Prince, and that he was from L.A., with this he had every girl's undivided attention. Going to L.A. and trying their hand at acting was the average dream in Déjà vu. Pharaoh didn't have to spend any money. The girls ordered and paid for his drinks, and the lap dances were free. Déjà vu became Pharaoh's second home. His V.I.P. table upstairs awaited him with a bottle of Don P chilling on ice. As soon as he sat down, girls started putting their bids in, each trying to outdo the other. Pharaoh enjoyed the competiveness and the extremes the girls were willing to go to in order to gain his attention. It reminded him of his ole' days of boss-ballin' up at 007.

The girl's weren't the only ones checking Pharaoh out. This white kid, maybe twenty-two at the most had been watching Pharaoh the past couple of days, and wondered how someone Pharaoh's age could afford to chill in V.I.P. everyday, all day. He did his homework on Pharaoh, asking certain girls about him, and where he's from. The only thing he was able to turn up was his name, Prince and that he was from L.A. "Excuse me, do you mind if I have a seat? I want to say something to you" the white boy said as he stood over Pharaoh's table."Ladies let me speak to this

man in private" Pharaoh said to the two dingy white chicks draped over his shoulders. They giggled after stealing a kiss from Pharaoh. He watched their soft backsides as they twitched away.
"My name's Barry," the guy said, extending his hand for Pharaoh's, but he just looked at it.
"Prince, what do you want?" Pharaoh was short with the suspicious looking young cracker. He had a thick French accent, but that meant nothing. He still could be them peoples.
"I just wanted to come over and introduce myself. I've been seeing you around lately and was wondering a few things" Barry said.
"Oh yeah, why you wondering about me? You the police or something?" Pharaoh asked, looking Barry over.
"Ha" laughed Barry. "The police" he repeated. "That's hilarious."
"Is it? You still haven't answered my question." Pharaoh knew that if he was in fact a cop, he'd have to say so, otherwise it would be deemed entrapment, depending on what business Barry was bringing Pharaoh's way.
"No, I am not a cop. I don't work for or with any law enforcement agency. I'm not a snitch, private investigator, none of the above. In fact, I believe we're both cut from the same cloth."
Pharaoh had to laugh at that one. Picture ole' whitey being cut from the same cloth as Pharaoh.
"What's so funny?" asked Barry.
"You," answered Pharaoh, in between laughs. "You and I can never be cut from the same cloth. God ran out of this material when he made me."
"I think you misunderstood me. What I meant is, we're both into the same things."
"Like what?"

"I've done my homework on you and I know just from talkin' to you that you're not from L.A. like you got everyone believing. There ain't but two types of dudes that roll through Windsor. Buffalo, New York and Detroit and you don't have a New York accent, so I'ma say you're from Detroit."
Pharaoh was amazed by how much game this pale face cracker had, his ability to pick up on that little bit of information. Being the street nigga that he was, Pharaoh didn't respond or admit to any of Barry's observations. "So, what do you want?"
"To perhaps do some business."
"I'm listening."
Barry dug in his jeans pocket and tossed Pharaoh a sandwich bag that was rolled up. Pharaoh could smell the stench of the bud fighting through the baggie before he even raised it to his face.
"30 levels of THC you're holding right there" Barry said, talking in lab terms.
Pharaoh didn't understand a word he just said. "This DRO'?"
"Yes, hydroponic."
Pharaoh pulled a long bud from the baggie and put it to his nose. "Yeah, this that exclusive," he said, admiring all the crystals.
"You ever smoke any?" asked Barry.
"Nah, I don't smoke." Pharaoh rolled the baggie up and tossed it back to Barry.
"You don't know what you're missing."
"And you showed me that because….?"
"I have lots of it. But I need someone to help me sell it."
"I ain't never worked for nobody my entire life."
"It's not like you'd be workin' for me, we'd be more like partners."

"I don't like that idea neither. How much a pound of that going for?"
"I usually won't sell pounds because it takes too much weighing and figuring."
Pharaoh wondered just how much DRO' this little cracker was sitting on. He had heard weed was legal in Ontario and other parts of Canada, but not to that extent. "Well, what do you sell?"
"I sell crops. The whole batch, whatever turns up is what I sell for a flat price."
"I'm lost" Pharaoh said.
"What I'm into is called cloning. You see that long bud you just pulled out? That's how I grow my stuff, all in single buds. I clone them using female buds. A crop may be two hundred pounds when I'm finished."
"What, you got like a warehouse where you doing all this?"
"I have a few locations."

Pharaoh nodded at the thought. Here he was sitting across from some geeky white boy who turns out to be a lab rat, cloning hydro plants. Pharaoh thought about if he set up a similar operation over in Detroit.
"What will you charge to teach me how to clone?"
"Two arms and both legs" Barry replied, as to say nothing. "In the words of Snoop Dogg, 'the game is not to be said, but hold'."
"I can respect that. A'ight, so how much for the crop then?"
"I'll give you this crop for $50,000."

Pharaoh's eyes lit up with dollar signs. He had to take a gulp of his Don P to hide the excitement. He was already adding up the profits 200 pounds for $50,000. One pound of hydro in Detroit cost $3,500 easy, and that's if you know somebody.
"I see you're adding up the profits," smiled Barry.
"Yeah, it sounds good, but what about getting it across the bridge?"

"That's not a problem, but I am willing to help if that's what it's going to take in order to make thing work out."
"I'm listening."
"I have a partner who leases boats. Instead of trying to make it across the bridge and taking a 50/50 chance of getting caught, we could use the water. My friend has speed boats, which we could use to meet up in the middle of the water and load the weed onto the other boat going back to Detroit."
"What about the Coast Guard?"
"It's all about timing. We speed out into international waters, toss the weed from one boat to the next, then both speed off in opposite directions. If the Coast Guard sees us, we'll drop the weed into the river. I have these steel cases that are waterproof. They'll sink straight down, leaving them with nothing. Then I'll send some of my guys to get them later on that night, because the cases have tracking devices on them."
"Man, that sounds like some *Mission Impossible* shit." Have you ever done this before?" asked Pharaoh.
"No. But I have done test runs, and each time we were able to pull it off. That's what's going to set up apart from all the other runners, assuming you're with me. We're doing something that the police aren't ready for. By the time someone tips them off, we'd been made millions on top of millions."
"I can see that," Pharaoh said, staring off into space. He really wanted to get back in the game, plus it would give Ralph and his crew motivation to knock the rest of his 'hit list' off.
"So, what do you think?"
"I like it. I just have one question, why me?" asked Pharaoh. He turned in his seat and looked Barry straight in his eyes,

"I told you. I believe we're both cut from the same cloth whether you want to believe it or not. I could have brought this to a number of guys, but I see something in you. I want to do business with you, Prince."
"Give me a number and a few days to think some things through, and I'll give you a call."
Barry scribbled his number onto a napkin, then handed it to Pharaoh. "Use it," he said, then slid his chair back and stood up.

Pharaoh looked at the napkin for a second, then tucked it safely inside his pimp pocket on his Evisul jeans. He reached for the bottle of Don P and took a long swig. He stared down at the naked women dancing on the stage and smiled. If Barry could do half of what he said, then Pharaoh's second run in the game was about to go down. Pharaoh could feel it.

Chapter Thirteen

Pharaoh called Ralph and told him that he wanted to see him and that it was important, lucky for Tone, which was the next nigga on the 'hit list.' Ralph and his crew were already gearing up to go get the nigga, but Pharaoh's call sounded urgent so Ralph stopped everything.

"I'm on my way," he said, hanging up the phone. He took off his black hoody and uncocked his 45, setting it on the table.

"Who was that?" Swift asked from the sofa. He was using a black scarf to load 9 mm shells into his 30 round clip Tech 9.

"Pharaoh. He wants to see me now. Not now, but right now," Ralph said.

"What about the vic?" asked Tuff.

"I guess he'll live to see another day. Ya'll take the day off and catch up on some NBA Live. I'ma go see what's up with, P."

"And while you over there, see wha's up with the castle he built us in the sky" J-Nutty snapped.

"For real, we out here killin' mo' niggas than slavery, and we ain't got shit to show for it. Not a single cent" Tuff mumbled.

"I'ma holla', just be cool," assured Ralph. He was tired of hearing his crew bitch and moan about not being paid for the work they were putting in.

In Ralph's mind, Pharaoh said he was gone hit they hand, and that was that. Ralph jumped in his Caprice and peeled out of the driveway. He sped down Gratiot Ave. hopping lanes, trying to beat the rush hour traffic. He wondered what could be so urgent that Pharaoh couldn't say over the phone. Ralph mashed the gas at the thought in a rush to get over to Canada. Within minutes he was crossing the Ambassador Bridge going over into Windsor. He flashed his phony passport and license at the border agent and was waved on.

Pharaoh was waiting for Ralph at the front door with two bottles of Cristal, one in each hand. He had this huge grin pulled back across his face like he didn't have a worry in the world. Ralph thought to himself 'damn, he must've already found Tez and killed him. What else could he be so damn happy about?' Ralph parked the car and got out.

"What up doe?" Pharaoh said, as he started down the array of stone steps. He handed Ralph one of the bottles, then embraced him with a half-hug.

"What you so geeked about? Tell me you didn't get him?" asked Ralph.

"Nah, I told you that I have faith in you. I'ma let you handle that" Pharaoh said.

"Then, what's the occasion?"

"Follow me." Pharaoh led the way around the side of the estate out to the back door where his brand new triple black cigar boat sat tied to the pier, rocking ever so gently against the waves.

"Where'd you get this?" Ralph asked.

"It was delivered this morning. Come on, get in."

"So, this was the big emergency?"

"Part of it," Pharaoh said as he started the engine. He hit the throttle a few times. The duel exhaust sounded like thunder and felt like an earthquake, all the vibrations going through their bodies.

"You sure you know what you're doing?" You know I'm too young to die," Ralph joked.

Pharaoh sat his bottle of Cristal down, then shifted the gears. The boat raised up in the front and skipped across the water like a rock. Ralph was glued to his seat as Pharaoh laid on the throttle. Within seconds they were at the shoreline of Belle Isle. Pharaoh made the boat fishtail for the on-looker, then did a donut and shot back to Windsor all in a matter of two minutes flat.

Pharaoh killed the engine and leaned back in his seat. He kicked his feet up on the dash, reached for his cigar case between the console and offered one to Ralph. He lit Ralph's cigar, then his own. "This is the life" Pharaoh said, blowing out a thick cloud of smoke. He watched as the smoke disappeared into thin air.

"P, what's up?" asked Ralph.

"You're what's up. It's your time to shine, and you can take your crew with you all the way to the top" Pharaoh said with a big grin.

"I like the sound of that. Tell me more" Ralph said, cheesin' from ear to ear.

"Ya'll been scratching names off that list like E-mothafucka, and it's time ya'll see some benefits behind ya'll work. I got a new connect on the weed, some DRO', and I want ya'll to push it."

"When?"

"We gone start tomorrow. But I just wanted to lace you on some things before we get started."

"Like what?"

"For one, I know yo' click ain't really the hustlin' type. Ya'll really head bustas. So, what I'ma do is coach ya'll from the side line. As long as niggas listen, we'll all make out."

"I feel you. So, how we 'pose to get the weed?"

"That's where the boat comes into play. You see how fast we shot over to Detroit and back? That's how. I already got it all set up. You gone have a boat coming from Detroit, while I'ma be coming from over here. We'll meet up in the middle, I'll toss ya'll the work, and then ya'll hit it back to the city. If the Coast Guard jumps on you, just throw the cases overboard. We'll come back and get that shit later."

"And where am I 'pose to get a boat from?"
"I told you, it's already set up. Here" Pharaoh said, handing Ralph a pair of binoculars. "Look to your right. You see that black speed boat across the water?"
"Yeah, I see it" Ralph said. "It looks just like this one."
"That's because it is. That's your boat. You'll have a driver with you, so don't even worry about that."
"How much weed we talkin' 'bout?"
"Two hun'd pounds."
Ralph set the binoculars down on the dashboard. He looked out into the water, then over at Pharaoh. "And just what am I 'pose to do with two hun'd elbows? Where I'ma see it at?"
"Calm down, Ralph. It aint nothin' but some weed. I got everything mapped out already. All you gotta do is follow the blueprint, and you and your niggas a be millionaires in a matter of months. We gone shut the city down."
"I just don't want to let you down, P. I don't wanna fuck up."
"And you won't. I believe in you" Pharaoh said, putting his arm around Ralph and pulling him to him. "It's your time. I did all the stuntin' I'm gone do. You up…"
Pharaoh's cell phone rang. He took his time answering because he wanted to let the caller ID register first. He recognized the number and smiled. "What the fuck up doe my nigga, my nucca" he answered, trying to sound excited.
"Fuck you mean what's up? Me being in here and you being out there is what's up." It was Ollie, and he was evidently pissed about something.
Pharaoh's smile vanished. He sat up and spoke. "My nigga, what done got into you, why you trippin' on me?" he asked.
"Cause nigga, like I said you're out there and I'm in here. You 'pose to take me with you. But nah, I didn't hear about

the shit until ten o'clock when they showed the shit on the news."

"My dude, you already know my first mind was to take you with me, but it would have been too hot on ole' girl's end to get us both MIA. It was hard as hell getting me, feel me?"

"Nah, I don't. I'm tired of sittin' on ice. I'm the only one still in jail just like the last time."

"And what I do last time? Got you the fuck up outta there, which is what I'm doin' right now as we speak. Nigga, I ain't gone never leave you stranded."

"So, when can I expect to come home 'cause these walls are biting?"

"I shot your mouthpiece some dust, and told him to file for a speedy trial."

"What? Why would you do that when I'll lose at trial?" asked Ollie.

"You say you've been watching the news, so you should know that shit is being handled. Trust me, you'll walk. You won't even have a trial."

"You make it sound so easy, but are you sure?"

"Don't ever doubt me, Ollie. You're coming home, and when you do it'll be you and me and my son right here" Pharaoh said, rubbing Ralph's head.

"I gotta go my nigga this battery going dead. P, don't leave me in here" Ollie pleaded.

Pharaoh could hear the worry in his voice. He felt bad for his friend because Ollie had been catching bad breaks. "I'm going all out for you my nigga. Just sit tight. I got a package coming to you and some bread."

"A'ight my nigga."

"One." *Click.*

"That was Ollie?" asked Ralph.

"Yeah… my nigga in there stressin' on me. That's why I need you to represent and get all them rat mothafucka's late, so my nigga can come home" Pharaoh said. He could see

Ollie lying across his bunk staring up at the ceiling stressing. He knew because he had spent many days and nights doing the same exact thing.
"I'ma tell you something, Ralph."
"I'm listening."
"Just because I'm putting you on with the weed doesn't mean I want ya'll slacking off. That list is number one priority. You got that?"
"I got you, P. It's gone get done. That's my word."

Pharaoh stared over at the sky-line of Detroit. Ollie's call had spoiled his good mood, not because he called, but because it made Pharaoh realize that he left his man behind. He had to go back for him. Ollie was the last real nigga standing beside Pharaoh. There was no way he could ever think about turning his back. Pharaoh meant it when he said that he was going all out, that meant even if he had to suit up and go hunt Tez down himself, it would be done. It was as if Ralph could read Pharaoh's mind. "We gone get him, P. Don't even trip" Ralph said. He raised his bottle of Cristal to Pharaoh's and clinked them together. "Ya' son got you" Ralph said proudly, then turned up his bottle. Pharaoh couldn't help but smile. He followed suit, turning up his bottle as well. He had a good feeling that everything would work out just fine.

Chapter Fourteen

"Man, we need to talk about what you gave me the other day" Peanut said.

"What's up?" Tez asked, he was talking on his cell phone while driving down 7 Mile Rd.

"I need you to come get this shit and bring my money with you" Peanut demanded.

"I don't do refunds, nigga. So, what's next?" asked Tez, cutting to the chase.

"Oh, so it's like that? You gone sell me some gank, that's for us?"

"Nigga, I don't know what the fuck you talkin' bout. You got it how I got it."

"Well, you needs to come take a look at this shit, and make my money right."

"Where you at?"

"On Justine."

"I'll see you in a minute." *Click.*

Tez tossed his cell phone in the side door panel and reached underneath his seat for his 40 cal. He cocked it, then put it in his waist. "I don't know who the fuck he think he was talkin' to" Tez said to himself. He punched down on the gas in a rush to get over to Peanut's spot.

Peanut was waiting on the front porch when Tez pulled up. Tez scanned the block for any of Peanut's people just in case the nigga had the heart to have somebody waiting on him. Unless niggas were hiding in the bushes or in the house, everything seemed to be normal. Tez got out of the car, leaving the key in the ignition and the doors unlocked in case he had to get low. Peanut had his ice-grill on as Tez climbed the three step porch.

"Where's the money?" asked Peanut.

"You gone get what's yours, I just want to see what the problem is."

Peanut snatched the screen open and held it for Tez. They stopped at the dining room table where Peanut had all the bricks spread out that Tez sold him the day before. All the bricks except two were busted opened.

"This shit ain't locking up when I try to cook it" Peanut said, waving his hand at all the bricks. "I done tried cookin' up from all these shits, and won't none of them jump back."

"You probably puttin' too much on it" Tez said as he inspected one of the open bricks.

"Nah, what it is, this shit ain't coke. This is some other shit."

"So, what you want me to do?" asked Tez.

"Ain't but one thing to do. You gotta make it right. I need mines."

"Yeah, you right." Tez stepped back and pulled his 40 cal. from under his hoody. "Come on Tez, man. We ain't gotta go like this. All I want is my money back" Peanut said, raising his hands while back stepping into the living room.

"Nah, you wanted me to make it right, so that's what I'ma do for you. I told you on the phone I don't do refunds, but here's your change."

Peanut tripped over the coffee table and landed on the sofa, that was his final resting place. Tez emptied the entire clip into his face and chest. He stood there long enough to watch Peanut's white –T turn dark red. Blood seeped from the blistering volcano holes down the sides of his body, staining the off-white leather sofa.

Tez walked out the house as if nothing even happened. He climbed in his car and cruised down the street. He slapped the dashboard and smiled while thinking back to Yacht. 'That bitch nigga was an ole' smart mothafucka,' he thought. Tez realized what Yacht had done. The money that Lil' One found in the safe turned out to be a Jewish Mint, a phony bankroll. Each stack had a hundred dollar bill on both ends, and in between were all singles, and it turns out that the 20 bricks were all dummies. Yacht was the coldest nigga to ever do it. He had the smarts to make up some fake bricks in case a nigga did ever get the ups on his, he'd have something to barter for his life. The plan was ingenious, but only one miscalculation. He didn't plan on running into a nigga like Tez who was going to kill him regardless. Tez took that one as a lesson learned. Check all money and bricks before you kill them. He laughed to himself. "I guess you can blame Yacht for you dying" Tez said, talking to Peanut. He was just tickled pink, either way it didn't make a difference to him. He sold each brick to Peanut for $5,000, so he and Lil' One were still sitting on a $100,000.

Tez slid through his hood to see what the word on the street was and to show his face to let niggas know he wasn't the one hiding. He pulled up to the basketball court on Syracuse and Hillsdale. There was a big time dice game jumping off in the middle of the court. Niggas from all over the city were in attendance, and not no peons. Tez knew there had to a least be a couple hundred grand in the game, and his asshole was itching to get out and lay all them niggas down. Only two things stopped him; one he was out of bullets, and two he didn't know if the feds were watching his block. Tez hit his horn, then rolled the window down. He stuck his head out the window to flag Floyd over. Floyd put his hand over his head like a visor and squinted to see who it was. He was leaning against his rusted out Delta '88.
"Let me see who this is" Floyd told, Ta'nae.
"Fuck you lookin' all around for? Get yo' scary ass in the car" Tez yelled.
"Ah, I ain't even know that was you. This you?" asked Floyd, as he climbed in the passenger seat.

"Something like that." No sooner than Floyd closed the door, Tez pulled off.
"What's up, where we going?"
"Bend a few corners" Tez said looking in his side mirror.
"Put it in the air."
"Look in the ashtray." Tez turned down Mound Rd. and relaxed. He cracked the sunroof and turned the radio on low.
"You know your name is ringing like E-mothafucka out here" Floyd said, after taking two pulls off the blunt."
"Oh, yeah." Tez looked over at Floyd.
"It's some lil' niggas runnin' around here asking 'bout you, like they tryna hit yo' head or something."
"Who is they?"
"I don't know. One of the lil' nigga's look familiar, but I can't put a name on it. And the feds be sittin' down on the corner watching yo' crib." Tez gripped the steering wheel tighter. His palms were getting sweaty, not because he was scared, but because he knew the feds weren't going to go away.
"Yeah, they be showing niggas yo' picture and shit, man. They on yo' ass" Floyd explained.

Tez pulled into Carney's Gun store on 8 Mile and Van Dyke. He and Floyd went inside so Tez could buy a couple of boxes of 40 cal. shells. They jumped back in the car heading back into the city. All the while, Tez was reloading his clip. Floyd continued on like a ten dollar snitch, giving up the word on the street.
"Oh, yeah," that's all Tez kept saying, as he listened to Floyd bump his gums.
"Who you know over there?" asked Floyd." Tez parked near an open field and cut the car off. "Come on," he said, pulling on the door handle.
Floyd's stomach did a back flip and rested in his ass. He didn't like the scenery, especially being out there with Tez.

"What..... what you ..... need me to do?" stuttered Floyd, as he followed a few steps behind Tez.

Tez made it to the middle of the field, then turned around fast with his 40 cal. in his hand.

"What I do, Tez? Man, we straight. I ain't got no beef with you..." Floyd pleaded his case. His heart was racing a mile a minute. There was no one to save him. The tall weeds hid them from any passing cars. Tez raised the gun to Floyd's chest and let off two shots. Floyd jerked then fell to the ground. He laid on his side twitching, still alive. Tez stood over him and put two slugs in his head. Tez listened to Floyd ramble on and on about how niggas and the feds were looking for him, and he wasn't about to take any chances. Floyd knew what type of car he was in, and in Tez's mind it would be a lot easier to just kill him versus having to buy a new car.

"I never liked you anyway. Bitch-made mothafucka" Tez said, mocking his idol, Nino Brown.

Tez walked back to his car and pulled off, leaving Floyd to the rats and other wild animals lurking nearby. Tez knew what he had to do in order for the streets to stop whispering, and for the feds to fall back. He had to find Pharaoh and kill him. This way, all speculation about him snitching on Pharaoh would cease because he wouldn't have to testify anymore, nor would he have to run from the alphabet boys anymore. He'd have his street-cred back, and his freedom. Tez liked the plan. He sat up in his seat and pushed down on the gas. "Yeah, that's what I'ma do" he said.

Chapter Fifteen

"Tony, maybe you leaving isn't such a bad idea. Do you really think that all those witnesses coming up dead, is just a coincidence?" Tone's momma asked him. They were sitting at the kitchen table at Tone's crib on Helen Street.

The feds told Tone that they wanted to put him in witness protection until they caught Pharaoh. Tone and Tez, were the last two besides Valdez who could really testify that they were buying weed from Pharaoh. Valdez's testimony alone by itself wouldn't be enough to prove a conspiracy.

"Ma, them crackers don't care nothin' about me. Whether I live or die, it makes them no difference. Tell me this. What's going to happen once all this is done and over?"

"They're offering you a new identity, secured job, and a house in a different state where nobody will know you."

"That means running. And once you start running, you'll be on the run for the rest of your life" Tone said.

"So, what are you going to do, Tony. I don't want to get no phone call in the middle of the night, saying that you've been killed. You're all I have, you and your brother."

"Ma, I promise that nothin' is going to happen to me. And I'm not running," assured Tone.

"I wish you'd change your mind, but on one hand you are your father's son, just like him too. Bull headed. Come on, and let me out," Ma' Dukes said, as she got up and grabbed her purse. She chewed Tone's ass all the way to the front door.

"I know. I love you too," Tone said, as he opened the front door. He stole a kiss from his mom, then let her out.

Despite all that, 'I'm not runnin' shit,' Tone was actually scared to death. He knew his number was up, but he held onto that thin thread of hope that just maybe he'd survive. He was so addicted to the streets of Detroit, that he didn't know how to leave, even though, he had violated in a major way. Tone looked up and down the block, while he stood in the door. As soon as his mom got in her car, Tone closed the door, put all four locks on and slid two boards over the door frame. Tone was on egg shells. Deep down, he knew that he was going to die soon, but it had to play itself out. Tone kicked back on the sofa in the front room and picked up the cordless phone. He called his baby's momma, Neese, and they started reminiscing about last night's booty-call. "That thang was wet…last night. What you was doing before you came over?" asked Tone, as he slid his hand down inside his boxer's. "Squats." Next time we gone see how many squats you can do on this dick…"

*****

"Yo, you ever wonder…" J-Nutty asked, then paused as he took two hits from the blunt that was in rotation. He continued his question as he blew out the smoke, his voice was groggy. "You ever wonder what goes through a nigga's mind right before he dies?"

"Shit, nigga be praying that his ass doesn't die," Swift said, taking the blunt from Tuff.

"Nah, I mean like, I think a nigga can feel it, when he's about to die. Whenever I kill somebody, I always look 'em in the eyes before I squeeze the trigger. I be lookin' at they soul" J-Nutty said.

"That's why they call you, J-Nutty. 'Cause yo' ass is crazy" Robin laughed.

"Nah, I think I see where you're coming from. I done seen mad niggas a day or two before they got killed, and when I think back on the looks on their faces – I can see death on them" Tuff said in agreement with J-Nutty.

"Kinda like how ole' boy was looking when he was standing on the porch, how he kept looking up and down the street" Swift said.
"Exactly. That's more than just him being paranoid. That's death on that nigga's face" Tuff explained.
Well, let's not disappoint him come on," said J-Nutty. He reached over Swift who was in the passenger seat of the stolen Expedition, and opened the glove box. J-Nutty hit the trunk button, and the hatch popped open.

Robin, Tuff and Swift were putting their blunts out and strapping up with their Ak-47's. J-Nutty got outof the truck and walked around to the hatch. He pulled the four Corona beer bottles out that he had filled with gasoline and stuffed rags in, making them into real live cocktails. Tuff, Swift and Robin slid out of the truck bearing their rifles. They each took a cocktail from J-Nutty. "A'ight, ya'll know the plan" Swift said, as he led the way across the street toward Tone's house. It was broad daylight, but those young, crazy niggas didn't care. They had enough shells to go to war with the entire police department. Swift lit his cocktail first and launched it through the front window of Tone's house. Robin, Tuff and J-Nutty lit theirs and surrounded the house.

*****

"What the fuck!" Tone yelled, as he jumped up from the sofa. The cocktail burst and fire spread across the drapes and carpet. "Baby, what's wrong?" Neese, Tone's baby momma asked frantically. Tone tried to run through the living room, but two cocktails crashed through the side windows. He looked at the back of the house, and another cocktail came flying through the kitchen window. "Baby, what's going on?" asked Neese. "Call the police, and tell 'em to get over her, now!" Tone yelled, then threw the phone down. He was surrounded by flames. The fire had spread to the walls and ceiling. Tone put his shirt over his face to block the smoke, then turned around in a circle looking for the best exit. The front door was his only option because flames had engulfed the back of the house and window ledges. Tone ducked low and charged through the blazing doorway leading to the front door. He fiddled with the locks, then snatched the boards down and opened the door. He choked and gagged as he stumbled out of the house onto the front porch.

Swift blind-sided, Tone as he leaned against the stone railing. *Laaka! Laaka! Laaka!...* Swift caught Tone in the left side of his rib cage, dropping him on the porch. Robin, Tuff and J-Nutty all ran around the front of the house. They all climbed the steps up to the landing of the porch. Tone was gasping for air, while holding his side. "See, that's the look I'm talkin' 'bout right there" J-Nutty said, pointing at Tone's face. They all raised their rifles from the side, and pointed dead at Tone. *Laaka! Laaka!....* They rocked Tone's ass to sleep, literally. The 223 shells were knocking patches out of Tone's body. When they stopped shooting, half of the nigga's face was blown off, and deep craters filled with blood covered his torso and legs. Satisfied with their kill, they all started down the steps and walked across the street, as if nothing had happened. An old man stepped outside onto his porch, and stared at them while they walked toward the Expedition. J-Nutty raised his AK at the man and started shooting. *Laaka! Laaka! Laaka!* The old man broke back into the house. "Get yo' old nosy ass in the house" J-Nutty yelled. They all bust out laughing, then climbed in the truck and smashed out. They ditched the Expedition on Strasburg and 7 Mile, and jumped in Ralph's Caprice. They drove back to the crib on Rosemary, where they all lived. Ralph was sitting on the porch when they pulled into the driveway. He had been waiting on them to get back. He couldn't wait to tell them what Pharaoh said.

"What up doe," Ralph said as he stood up.

"What the nigga say?" asked Swift, as he climbed the steps. Robin, Tuff and J-Nutty were right behind him. They were all ears.

"We 'bout to start getting this money" Ralph said with a smile.

"Nigga, when? We been hearing that same line for too long. We just stanked ole' boy. So, when we gone start eating?" asked Tuff.

"In a few days. Check this out," Ralph said as he tossed Tuff the jar of Hydro Pharaoh had given him. "That's what we gone be selling, p-o-u-n-d-s" Ralph emphasized the word 'pounds.'

"This that drizzle-dro," Tuff said after smelling the jar. He passed it to Swift, who was standing beside him.

"Yeah, this that official tissue," Swift seconded.

"Pharaoh is going to let us do our thing. He said that we done proved our loyalty, so let's keep proving it by knocking the rest of these niggas' heads off. We can get a lot more done, if we were to split up in groups of two. But we gotta finish what we started. The money ain't going nowhere. We gone eat, shine, stunt and all that other shit, but we gotta take care of this business" Ralph said.

"Who next on that list?" asked Tuff.

"Shit, anyone of them shits will do" Ralph replied. "We just need to get 'em done." He flipped open his phone and texted Pharoah: five down…

Tuff bust a blunt down and cracked the jar open on the hydro. Robin, Swift and J-Nutty all stood over Tuff's shoulder as he poured the buds inside the blunt and crumbled them with his thumb and index finger. He twisted the blunt and licked the seal, then waved a lighter underneath the seal. "Look at ya'll niggas. Ya'll look like a bunch of crackheads," laughed Ralph. Tuff sparked the L,

took two pulls, then passed it to Swift. Tuff savored the smoke in his lungs before exhaling smoke through his nose.
"How that shit hit?" asked Ralph.
"Nigga, we bout to shut the city down with that," Tuff said, in between coughs. Ralph smiled. That's exactly what he needed to hear.

Chapter Sixteen

The night lights of the Ambassador Bridge gleamed across the Detroit River, providing the only means of light, with the exception of a few scattered stars in the sky. Pharaoh and Barry figured at night would be the best time to make their move. They sat at the dock with the boating idling. Pharaoh called Ralph's cell while he looked straight across the water through a pair of binoculars.

"Ya'll niggas ready?" asked Pharaoh.

"Waitin' on you" Ralph said.

"A'ight, just like we planned it."

"I got you." *Click.*

Pharaoh climbed out of the boat and let Barry take the wheel. Barry's right hand man, Jeff, climbed in the boat, so he could help toss the cases over to Ralph's boat. Barry shot away from the dock like a bat out of hell. He had the exhaust silenced so not to alert the Coast Guard. The blackness of the boat made it impossible to see it moving. Barry and Jeff were dressed from head to toe in all black with ski masks on. This was Pharaoh's idea. He made Ralph and his crew wear them as well, so that nobody could identify the next man. Ralph pulled alongside Barry's boat in the same exact cigar boat. "Let's go, let's go," Barry ordered, while looking in all directions, his voice was muffled from the mask. "Thirty seconds," he said. "Last one" Jeff announced, as he tossed Swift the last case. Without saying another word, both boats did a u-turn and punched it back to their sides of the river. Pharaoh smiled as he watched Ralph pull up to his dock, and his team unloading the black steel cases from the boat into an awaiting van. It worked, and would continue working long as everybody stayed on point. The shit took less than two

minutes to make $650,000. That was the feeling that Pharaoh missed. He got his high off of making money, lots of it. Barry pulled back up to the dock and killed the engine. Pharaoh helped him out of the boat and gave him some dap with a smile.
"That shit worked" Pharaoh said with a big grin on his face.
"I told you it would," smiled Barry. Pharaoh already had three victory bottles on ice. He dug down in the Igloo cooler and handed Barry and Jeff a bottle of Cristal. They all popped the corks and clinked their bottles together.
"To the good life" Barry cheered.
"I'll drink to that any day" Pharaoh said. He was already plotting the second run. Pharaoh felt alive again, like he was back in the game. He was living through Ralph, trying to relive his glory days. He gave Ralph the blueprint from start to finish on what to do and how to set up. All Ralph had to do was follow the plan and get rich.

Meanwhile Ralph and Swift split off from J-Nutty, Robin and Tuff. Pharaoh gave Ralph specific instructions on where to take the weed, and who to take with him. He told him to only take his right hand, Swift with him. The rest of them, Pharaoh said to leave in the dark.
Ralph pulled the van into an alley on Bloom St. directly behind an abandoned warehouse. It was one of Pharaoh's old stash spots. He still owned the place and the feds had never found anything there, so he figured it was still a good spot to use. Ralph got out of the van and walked around to the garage door. He fiddled with some keys in the headlights of the van. He tried every key on the ring in the rusted pad lock. Finally, on the last key he got it open. Ralph reached down for the lever and raised the sliding door up. A ton of rats raced out of the warehouse splitting up down the alley. Ralph felt around the wall for a light switch. He found two, but neither did anything, so he

climbed back in the van and pulled inside the garage leaving his lights on.
"Close the door," Ralph said to Swift.
"Nigga, is you blind, you ain't see all them fuckin' rats come runnin' out of here" Swift whined.
"Bring yo' scary ass on, my man" ordered Ralph. He got out and went straight to work. There were twenty cases in all, each containing ten pounds of DRO'.
"Leave two cases in the van" Ralph said as he carried three cases over to a huge wall locker. He put the cases on the top shelves so the rats wouldn't have a field day eating the shit.
"Why we leaving it here?" asked Swift.
"Where else we gone keep it?" asked Ralph.
"At the crib. I think it's a lot safer over there, than to leave it in this musty ass warehouse."
"And that's exactly why we're leaving it here, because nobody's gone suspect nothin' to be in here. But what about when we start gettin' money, niggas gone be plottin' cause we gone be shining too hard."
"I feel you," nodded Swift.
"And another thing is this, we're the only two that knows where the work is at, you, me and Pharaoh. So, it should be safe."
"What about Tuff, Robin and J-Nutty?"
"If I wanted them to know, I wouldn't have gone through all this. They would be standing here with us. I showed you because you're my right hand. They crew, but they my left hand. Feel me?"
"Yeah, I feel you," smiled Swift.
"Nigga, we 'bout to get this money. All the days of sittin' up fantasizing about it is over. It's here, all we gotta do is go get it." "Come on, we out." He and Swift locked the warehouse up and climbed in the van to go meet up with the rest of the crew.

Chapter Seventeen

Ralph had done everything Pharaoh told him to do, as a result, everything was coming together. Ralph positioned DRO' houses all on the east side. He and Tuff, Robin and J-Nutty were overseeing the houses, each of them was responsible for the workers under them. They had to pay them to make sure the weed was jarred up at its proper weight, 1 gram cost $20. Tuff, Robin, and J-Nutty each had four houses under them, on average each house was doing three pounds a day. Word hit the streets that the drizzle with the white crystals was on deck, and niggas went crazy, especially the niggas who were getting any type of money. They'd pull up to the spot and spend no less than $100. Niggas would ask for twenty jars, and that's just one dude. All the money getters would come fill up before they hit the club, hotel, or if they were going out of town. Niggas was loving the DRO' so much, they wouldn't smoke anything but the DRO', and it had to have them crystals.

It had been less than a month and the 7 Mile Dawgz were starting to ring bells in the streets. Everybody was talking about these lil' young niggas who had the DRO'. Tuff, Robin, and J-Nutty dropped three chargers. Ralph and Swift kept jumping in different rentals everyday. Ralph wanted to do it big how Pharaoh and Tez did it with the 600's, but he had to stack his money first. Off every pound, Ralph had to give Pharaoh $1,500. So, it was like Pharaoh was only making $500 off every pound. He was really just doing it to keep Ralph and his lil' niggas happy and ready to kill something at his command. Ralph lived on his cell. He was busy making contacts with niggas in lil' hick towns like Grand Rapids, Saginaw, Flint and Adrian, Michigan. Pharaoh was calling the plays from his cigar boat. He told

Ralph to hit up all those little spots and dump some work on them niggas. He said that Ralph could charge them out of town prices, $5,000 a pound. So far, Ralph was making his rounds. He and Swift were on their way to Madison, Wisconsin. They had never been there before. They knew nothing about the spot, other than it was supposed to be a lot of money out there, and a bunch of fine white bitches

Swift pulled into the BP Gas station on Caniff. Ralph told him to pull in the station after seeing a bunch of black dudes getting out of a Green Geo Storm. It was so many niggas packed in that car, that it looked like one of those clown cars from the circus. "Pull up right here" Ralph said. Swift parked near these two white chicks sitting at the pump. They smiled at Swift as he looked down from the Navigator at them. Ralph got out of the truck and stepped inside the gas station. He grabbed a bottle of water from the cooler and stepped to the end of the line. "Oh, you can go head, Joe," a dude looked at Ralph and said. He was in the middle of four other dudes and was telling them a story. Ralph paid for his water and bought Swift a box of Swiser's. He was thinking of a way to cut into the group of niggas standing behind him. The man who had been telling the story saw the cashier hand Ralph the box of blunts.

"A, Joe," he said.

Ralph turned to face him, "what up, doe?"

The man squinted his eyes and tried to remember where he had heard that slang before. "Where you from, Joe?" he asked, Ralph.

"Detroit."

It hit the man, that's where he had heard the slang 'what up doe.' "Okay I just left some of your homies in the penn. You know Freddy Mason?"

"Nah".

"Real good dude. He was in Tarre Haute with me. But anyway, you got something to blow on? I see you got the L's."
"Holla at me outside". Ralph grabbed his water and the box of Swiser's, and led the way outside.
"They call me Sean-G" the man said, extending his hand as they stepped outside.
"Where you from?" Ralph asked, shaking the man's hand.
"I'm from the Chi. I just come up here with the folks and hustle."
"Who?" asked Ralph, as he and Sean-G walked toward the Navigator.
"The folks, GD's" Sean-G explained. He could tell that Ralph didn't know what the hell he was talking about, so he left it alone. "Ya'll nigga's riding slick, ain't ya'll?" asked Sean-G.
Ralph opened the passenger door to the cranberry red Navigator. He tossed the Swiser's on Swift's lap, who was still leaning out the window rapping to the white chicks. "Here, check this out," Ralph said. He handed Sean-G a jar of DRO' from the console.
Sean-G's eyes got big as he raised the jar to eye level. "This that monkey right here," he said, unscrewing the cap. "Yeah…." he said, after sniffing the funky jar. "What you want for this?"
"It's yours. It's a sample."
"Good lookin'. But I know the shit is official. I'm tryna' get some more of this before ya'll leave. All these niggas got around here is some dirt. I don't smoke, but I know that I'll kill 'em with these," Sean-G said.
"You got five stacks?" asked Ralph.
"Why what's up?" asked Sean-G.
"That's what I'm letting pounds go for."
"I'ma be real with you, Joe. I don't have no five stacks. I'm that nigga everybody comes to when they tryna' off

something or tryna' cop something. I can help you dump a few, and you just look out on the back end" Sean-G explained.
"I tell you what. For every pound you help me get rid of, I'ma give you a stack off the top" Ralph explained.
"That's love," Sean-G said cocking his hand back for a play. "Where ya'll staying at?" he asked.
"We're not. We just sliding through, tryna' make some contacts, then we back on the road."
"Well, look. I'ma shoot around the corner and holla at this lame nigga, Tate. I know he gone want at least three."
"A'ight, we'll be right here," Ralph said, then climbed inside the truck.
"My man," Ralph said, nudging Swift.
"What? Nigga, I'm tryna' linc something up with these hoes" Swift snapped.
"Well, tell them to pull across the street to the Burger King." Swift had the white chicks follow them across the street. "Park near the back," Ralph instructed.
"What the fuck you got us on?" asked Swift.
"On money, nigga. What else?"

Ralph climbed in the back seat and pulled the door panel off to the back door. He reached down and pulled out three pounds of compressed DRO' wrapped in Reynolds wrap out from the panel, and tucked them under the seat. Swift motioned to the two white chicks to get in the truck. They giggled as they climbed inside the Navigator.
"This my brother, Ralph," Swift said introducing them all. Both of the girls were thick as shit, fat asses, little waists and flat stomachs. One was seated up front with Swift, and the other one was in the back with Ralph.
"I'm saying, ya'll smoke weed?" asked Swift.
"No" answered the girl in the passenger seat.
"Well, what do ya'll do besides giggle?" asked Swift.
The girls looked at each other and giggled again.

"Have ya'll eve been with a black man before?" asked Swift.

"No…" said the passenger.

Ralph was watching the BP Gas station. He was waiting for Sean-G to pull back up. He looked down at the white chicks hands, she was unfastening his pants. Ole' girl in the front seat was already leaned over with Swift's dick in her mouth. Ralph felt the warmth of the girl's mouth, as she went down on him. Here it was, they just met these two chicks and they were sucking their dicks already. 'It must be the Navigator,' Ralph told himself while loving every minute of it. This chick was a head specialist; she found her rhythm and stuck to it. She sucked down on the head, as Ralph shot off in her mouth. "Hmmm…" she moaned, as if the cum tasted good in her mouth. Ralph pulled the girl up and fastened his pants. He saw the Geo Storm pull back into the BP station. Swift got the girls' number before putting them out.

"I'ma call you" he promised.

"Fuck these hoes, pull over to the station," ordered Ralph.

Sean-G was standing in front of the BP looking around. He smiled at the sight of the Navigator pulling in. "Where you go?" he asked.

"Across the street to get something to eat. That's yo' man in the car?" Ralph asked, nodding toward the Geo.

"Yeah, but you ain't gotta meet the nigga. He just wanted to come I guess to watch his money."

"Oh, that's cool. I got the shit right here. You three, right?" Ralph asked, as he reached in the backseat.

"Yeah" Sean-G answered. He was looking real shifty, and Swift noticed.

As Ralph pulled the three pounds from under the backseat, Sean-G came out of the Foot Action bag he was carrying with a chrome 38. Ralph turned around with the pounds in his hand and jumped back. "Nigga, you know what it is," Sean-G said pointing the gun dead at Ralph's stomach. The passenger who was sitting in the Geo jumped out with his hand underneath his shirt and walked around the back of the truck. Swift was slowly raising his 45 on the side of the seat, while looking in his side mirror at ole' boy. The nigga snatched the driver's door open and tried to pull out from under his shirt, but Swift gave it to him. *Boom! Boom!* Swift jumped out of the truck and stood over the nigga and aired his ass out. *Boom!...* Sean-G bust, Ralph in the stomach once, then grabbed the three pounds and got little on foot. *Boom! Boom! Boom!* Swift took three shots at Sean-G and missed. Swift ran around to the passenger side of the car, where Ralph laid clutching his stomach. His hands were covered with blood. "Come on, my nigga. I got you. Just don't die on me," Swift said, as he stuffed Ralph in the backseat. He ran around the truck and jumped in. He peeled out of the parking lot of the gas station, not knowing where it was he was going. "Ralph!" Swift yelled, then looked back at Ralph. "Yeah" Ralph said in a low tone of voice. "Keep yo' eyes open, my nigga. I'ma get you to the hospital." He flipped open his cell phone and called the two white chicks they had just met. They gave him directions to the hospital and told Swift they'd meet him there. "I got you, my nigga. Don't die on me" Swift yelled. He read the signs on the streets, as he floored the Navigator.

Swift flew into the entrance of the emergency room. He pulled the nose of the Navigator up to the sliding doors and jumped out. He pulled Ralph from the back of the truck and put him over his shoulder. "I got you, my nigga. You hear me, Ralph?" "Yeah," Ralph said faintly.

Swift rushed through the sliding doors with Ralph over his shoulder. "Oh, my God. Is he still alive?" one nurse asked, rushing over to attend to Ralph. "Sit him on this stretcher over here," she ordered. She clicked her fingers, and her emergency team fell into play. They surrounded Ralph, lifted the stretcher and rushed off with him. Swift tried following behind Ralph, but was stopped at the operating room door. “Doc, please don’t let him die. That’s all I got right there,” Swift said, becoming teary-eyed. “We will do our very best,” answered the doctor. He slapped Swift on the shoulder, then joined his team. Swift paced the waiting room floor with revenge on his mind and hate in his heart. Before they left, Swift told Ralph that he had a bad feeling something was going to happen, but Ralph insisted on taking the trip. He wanted to show Pharaoh that they were moving big numbers and expanding into other states.“I told you…” Swift said.

The two white girls raced into the emergency room. Is he okay?” asked the one who had sucked Ralph’s dick earlier. She sounded like she was his wife or girlfriend.

“I don’t know. They just took him in” Swift mumbled.

“Oh, my God. What happened, we just left you guys?” Swift’s girl asked.

“Did ya’ll see the guy Ralph was talking to at the gas station? The one in the lil’ Geo?” asked Swift.

“Yeah that’s Crazy.”

“Ya’ll know where he be at?” asked Swift.

“He’s all over Madison, but he’s from Chicago. Why, was Crazy the one who shot Ralph?”

“Nah, nah,” lied Swift.

The doctor stepped into the waiting room and motioned Swift to step over to the desk. “I have some papers for you to sign.”

“Fuck them papers. What’s the status on my brother?” demanded Swift.

“We need to perform surgery. Before we can do that, I need for you to sign a waiver.”

“I’m not waiving nothing,” Swift yelled.

“Listen, son. Your brother doesn’t have insurance, and he needs surgery. The only way I can operate on him, is if you

sign a waiver saying that in the event something goes wrong, the hospital or myself won't be liable."
"And if I don't?"
"Then, your brother will certainly die on the stretcher he went in on."
Swift signed the forms and handed them back to the doctor. He grabbed the doctor by the arm, "If my brother dies, you won't have to worry about no lawsuit." Swift released the doctor, then returned to where the white chicks were standing.
"What did he say?" one of them asked.
"He going into surgery."

Chapter Eighteen

Swift spent the night in the waiting room of the hospital. The two white chicks kept him company. They were all curled up on the hard plastic chairs asleep. The doctor who performed Ralph's surgery was at the front desk talking to a nurse, who pointed in the direction of Swift and the girls. The doctor approached the group.

"Excuse me," he said, tapping Swift's leg.

Swift's eyes popped open, and he sat up while pulling his arms out of sleeves. "Tell me something good, Doc. Is he okay?"

"He's just fine. He pulled through surgery with no complications. We were able to locate the bullet, and stop the internal bleeding."

"Can I see him now?" asked Swift.

"He's resting. But I'll allow you to visit him for a few minutes. Follow me." Swift and the girls followed the doctor through the emergency room into the Intensive Care Unit. "He's right in there" the doctor said, waving his hand at the doorway.

Swift slowly walked inside the room and tried to brace himself for the worst. He stepped around the curtain and saw Ralph laid up in bed with his eyes closed. Swift walked around the side of Ralph's bed, and just looked at his best friend for a minute. "We'll be out in the hall," one of the girls said, as they excused themselves. Swift picked Ralph's hand up. He closed his eyes and started talking. "My nigga, I told you we should've stayed at the crib. You tryna' do too much too fast. Ain't no amount of money worth any of us dying. I know you want to show P. that we can handle the business, but it ain't just about him. We need you. I need you."

"You sentimental ass nigga," Ralph laughed. Swift opened his eyes, and dropped Ralph's hand.

"What, you don't want to hold my hand no more?" Ralph teased. He had been looking at Swift the entire time he was talking.

"Fuck you nigga. I'm just making sure you're alright" Swift said, trying to put his gangsta' face back on.

"I'm just fuckin' with you. You know, you're my nigga" Ralph said.

"Yeah, well I meant what I said. You need to slow down and let the money come to us. Look at you, a nigga almost killed you over three funky-ass pounds."

"I'ma fall back. But tell me you didn't call home and tell nobody I got shot?" asked Ralph.

"Nah, I knew you wouldn't want Pharaoh to get word."

"You think you know me, huh?" asked Ralph.

"Like E-mothafucka. So, when did the doctor say you can leave?" asked Swift.

"Shit, he didn't. But I'm ready to dip now. I can get these staples taken out at the crib" Ralph said, as he pulled the covers off him.

"You sure?" asked Swift.

"Yeah. I need to get back to the city and…"

"And what?" What, take care of Pharaoh's little list?"

"Yeah," Ralph said, as he tried to stand up, but pain shot through his stomach.

"Hold on. 'Cause you 'bout to kill yo' self" Swift said. He stepped in the hallway and told the girls to bring him a wheelchair.

"Who was that?" asked Ralph.

"Oh, them two white bitches from the gas station. They say the nigga who shot you goes by the name, Crazy. They can help find the nigga, so we can stank him. Then we can stank they ass, too."

"Fuck that shit" Ralph snapped. He was fumbling around for his clothes. "Where the fuck are my clothes?" he asked.

"What you mean, fuck that shit? I know you ain't gone just let that shit ride? That nigga almost killed you, and he cold disrespected us," Swift said.

"We ain't have no business out here in the first place, not fucking with his thirsty-ass no way. So, let's just take it as a loss and go home. We don't have time to be on one fuckin' man hunt for some bumb-ass nigga named, Crazy. It is, what is it."

"Yeah, I know what it is" Swift mumbled, as he walked to the door. The girls were back with the wheelchair.

"Are you okay?" Ralph's girl asked him, as she put the brakes on the chair.

"Yeah. I'm cool. Let's get out of here before they try and tell me I can't leave."

Chapter Nineteen

Meanwhile, Jeff, Robin, and J-Nutty were making it rain at 007. They each had two hands full of ten dollar bills. They were pouring them onto the two strippers that were on stage.

"I'm rich, bitch. I'ma real big tymer" they all shouted, as Baby and Mannie Fresh's song dropped into the hook. "Gator boots, with the pimped out Gucci suits. Ain't got not job, but I stay sharp…" Tuff, Robin, and J-Nutty were popping their collars, and talking cash money shit to the strippers. "Boss up, and get this money, bitch" J-Nutty yelled. He was buzzin' good and feelin' himself.

"You fuckin' or what?" Tuff asked one stripper.

"Yeah, bitch. If you ain't fuckin', we ain't fuckin' with you," added Robin.

They were all in what they called in Detroit, Boss Mode. They said whatever came to mind, and didn't give a fuck who liked it.

"Bitch, get us some mo' bottles over here," Tuff ordered.

Chyna was working as the bar maid that night. She started to cuss Tuff's young ass out, but she caught herself. She knew that they were just some youngins who had just started getting money. They were just trying to make a name for themselves. She went to the bar and got them three more bottles of Cristal, then took them over to the stage. "Here you go" Chyna said. She popped the corks, and allowed J-Nutty to tuck his tip in her garter belt.

"Damn, baby girl. I love to pop yo' cork," J-Nutty said, looking Chyna up and down.

"Boy, please… you are too young for me" Chyna was abaout to walk away, but J-Nutty reached for her hand.

"My money is old, though. And I don't mind trickin' a lil' off, long as it's worth it" J-Nutty bragged.
"Chyna looked, J-Nutty over. "I'll think about it. Now can I get back to work?" she asked.
J-Nutty let go of Chyna's hand and watched her as she walked away. "You won't know what to do with all that ass" Robin said.
"Shit, I'll put my face in it" J-Nutty shot back.
"You nasty-ass nigga," laughed Tuff.
"Shit, I ain't gone lie. I'd probably have to taste that too."
They all bust out laughing, and clinked their bottles together.
"Lil' One, come here," Tez whispered from his private V.I.P. booth near the back of the club. He motioned Lil' One over to the table as she came out of the dressing room.
"What's up, baby?' How come you ain't tell me you were coming, I could have had a plate ready? asked Lil' One.
"I wasn't planning to, but I was driving past and saw that it was packed. I couldn't miss the opportunity to jack one of these niggas."
"Tez, I thought you were going to relax for a little while, and enjoy some of the money."
"I tried to. But you know how I get when I'm bored," Tez said. "Besides killin', you the only thing that can keep me calm," he said, kissing on Lil' One's chest.
"Hmm, hm."
"But tell me, who are them three niggas right there?" asked Tez. He was looking at Tuff, Robin, and J-Nutty over by the stage.
"I don't know. They keep hollerin' 7 Mile Dawgz, I guess that's the name of their click. Why, you thinking about getting 'em, baby?" asked Lil' One.
"Shit, if I don't another nigga will. I might as well. See what you can find out about them lil' niggas. I want to

know what it is they're selling and where they from" Tez said.
"7 Mile Dawgz, huh? Let's see how much of a dawg you are when you're staring down the barrel of my 40," Tez said, as he watched Lil' One go to work.

Lil' One slid right up under Robin, and went to giving him a lap dance. Lil' One had become a pro at seducing niggas and setting them up for the kill. Her flawless body made it impossible for any man to resist her advances. She mounted Robin's lap and did her number. She looked over Robin's shoulder and smiled at Tez. "That's right, baby. Work that nigga..." said Tez.

Chapter Twenty

"So, what you want me to tell the crew? You kow they gone be asking about you," asked Swift. He had just dropped Ralph off at his new apartment in Haper Woods, Michigan behind Eastland Mall.

'I don't want you to tell 'em nothing. Ask 'em how many niggas have they scratched off that list" Ralph said. He was stretched out on the sofa in the living room.

"How long you think you'll be out of commission?" asked Swift.

"I gotta get these fuckin' staples taken out, so I say about a week."

"A'ight, my nigga. You just kick back and let me handle the B.I."

"Remember what I said, Swift. Don't tell nobody what went down. I just wanna forget it ever happened."

"I got you. I'm getting ready to dip. You need anything before I go?"

"Nah, I'm straight. Just handle that list and keep the money straight."

"A'ight. Call me if you need something," Swift said, giving Ralph a play, then let himself out.

Ralph flipped open his cell phone and pushed the send button. He wanted to call Pharaoh, but didn't feel like hearing Swift's mouth. "What up doe?" asked Ralph. He broke a wide smile at the sound of Pharaoh's voice. "Yeah, everything's good. Just calling to check on you. Today, I don't think I'ma be able to make it today. I gotta meet up with a few niggas, you know how that shit is. Tomorrow, I don't know either… I tell you what, next week I'ma slide through and fuck with you. But I gotta still tie up a few loose ends on that demo. Yeah, but, uh I was just checking you out. I'ma fuck with you later. A'ight. One." *Click.* Ralph turned his phone off completely and laid back on the sofa. He was fucked up that he just lied to Pharaoh. He felt like he had more respect for him than that, but he couldn't tell Pharaoh that he'd been shot by some out of town nigga over three pounds. Ralph felt like he'd be disappointing Pharaoh because he had schooled him better.

*****

"Who was that, baby?" asked Stacy. She and Pharaoh were kicked back on the cigar boat enjoying the cool breeze coming off the water.

"That was my lil' man, Ralph. You remember the one who used to come see me at the county?"

"Okay, how's he doing?"

"He's doing good. I love that lil' nigga like a son. He's the one helping me get my life back. Pharaoh said. He looked across the water at the city. Being in Canada was cool, but Pharaoh started feeling like he was still in jail. He couldn't go back to Detroit, or the United States unless he had wiped that list out.

"What are you thinking about?" Stacy asked. She could see that look in Pharaoh's eyes.

"I just want my life back." Pharoah was thinking about his son, Jr. Pharaoh hadn't seen Jr. since he walked out of the courtroom, and Ma' Dukes held him up to say hi. That memory brought a brief smile to Pharaoh's face, but was replaced by a grimacing stare.

"It's going to work itself out," Stacy said. She lifted Pharaoh's arm, then curled up under him.

Pharaoh was getting mixed signals from Stacy. She was there for him, and had even helped him escape, but he felt like she was holding back like she didn't believe that they would have a happy ending. He needed Stacy. "Stacy, let me ask you something."

"What is it, baby?" asked Stacy. She was rubbing Pharaoh's chest. Together they looked out on the water.
"Do you think what I'm doing is far- fetched?"
"What do you mean?" asked Stacy.
"Me trying to erase the past, so that we can have a future. What I'm asking you is whether or not you believe in me?"
"Pharaoh," Stacy said, sitting up. "Of course I believe in you. But do I believe your ideals are a little far-fetched? Yes."
"So, you don't see a future for us, that's what you're telling me?" asked Pharaoh.
"I didn't say that."
"I want to be clear. Let's stop talking in riddles, and just put it all on the table."
"Pharaoh, I didn't come over here on my day off to argue. I came to relax."
"That's exactly what I'm talking about. You treating this as just a weekend rendezvous, like you're expecting the worst. What happens if I do go back, will that be the end of us, Stacy?" Pharaoh looked deep into Stacy's eyes. No words needed to be spoken. Pharaoh had gotten the answer he needed. "You love me, but you don't believe in me".

Pharoah leaned back in his seat and stared up at the stars in the sky. He had a helluva dilemma. He loved Stacy more so for what she had done for him, helping him escape, but Pharaoh had to put it all in perspective. 'Is this the extent of our relationship?' he asked himself. 'Maybe I love her because she got me out of jail. Could I see myself in love with her had she not helped me?' Pharaoh looked at Stacy, and the answer was yes. He really loved her, he knew that if he ever was going to live a normal life with Stacy, his far-fetched plans would have to come to pass. He couldn't fathom the flip side of the coin: life in prison.

Chapter Twenty-One

"Listen to me, my nigga. Tell your lawyer that you're not waiving the speedy trial rights. Don't sign no continuance."

"P, how you gone tell me to go to trial, when you're out there laid up drinking Crist and getting pussy. Dawg, you left me in this bitch for dead…"

"Ollie, you don't mean that."

"When we hit the bizank, I sat tight and kept solid, didn't I?"

"Yeah."

"I'm the only one out of our whole indictment that's still in jail." Ollie was kicked back in his cell talking on the cell phone Stacy brought him.

"Nigga, you act like I'm out here just sitting on my hands. When you fell last time, who made sure the proper heads got hit in order to get you home? I made sure yo' Ma' Dukes got your share of the bread, and I kept us a family despite all the bullshit Tez put us through. I know you've been watching the news…"

"Yeah," Ollie mumbled.

"Okay, then. That's my work. That's me out here making all these moves. So, when I say file for speedy trial, there's a reason behind it. Who's gone be there to take the stand on you? Tez is still on the run, and the rest of them niggas are no longer with us. When the prosecutor hears that you filed for a speedy trial, they gone shit on they self 'cause they don't have a case right now. And it's going to be a race against the clock."

"And what if they win?"

"How can he?"

"What if they catch Tez, or he turns himself in, then what?" asked Ollie.
"First of all, you know Tez as well as I do. That nigga ain't turning himself in to nobody. I don't even know why the nigga ran in the first place. But I know one thing, he's not going to let them catch him…" said Pharaoh.
"Yeah, but what if…"
"Ollie, have I ever lied to you?"
"No."
"Okay, then. I'm not about to start either. I'm giving you my word, on Jr.'s life that I'ma find the nigga before they do. And when I do, it'll be a sad day for his mom and kids. I know you're pressed to get out, and you tired of sitting, but it's all part of the game. The part nobody wants to deal with, which is why we're in the situation we're in now. Remember this and I'ma let you go. It's always gone be hard on a playa' when a sucka's around. Real niggas gone always have it hard. It ain't fair, but it is what is. My nigga, you stay solid and do what I told you. I'm on my job out here. You should be home in no time" Pharaoh said confidently.
"I hope so…cause this shit here is getting old," Ollie replied.
"A'ight. I'ma fuck with you later. Oh yeah, I gave Stacy a few G's for you, so you can do your thang."
"Good-lookin' my nigga."
"A'ight…"
"Pharaoh. Don't leave me in here…"
"I got you…a'ight, one." *Click.*

Pharaoh hung up the phone. He sat down at the kitchen table and stared at the hit list on the refrigerator. Tez's name had a bulls-eye around it and five stars next to it. Ollie's last sentence was stuck in Pharaoh's head. 'Don't leave me in here….' "I got you, my nigga. Just hold tight" Pharaoh said, as if he was talking to Ollie.

Pharaoh pulled his cell phone out of his pants pocket and called Ralph.
"Hello," answered Ralph.
"What up doe. We still on for today or what?" asked Pharaoh.
"Oh, shit. It is Monday, ain't it," Ralph said, looking at his watch. He was at the hospital, waiting to have his staples removed. 'Yeah, um…give me a couple hours and I'll be through there."
"A'ight. If I'm not in the house, I'll be out on the boat."
"A'ight. See you in a minute." *Click.*
Ralph hung up the phone, and walked over to the nurse who had been calling his name.
"Are you Hathaway?"
"Yes" Ralph answered.
"Right this way." The nurse escorted Ralph into a small exam room. "You can have a seat right there, this won't take but a few minutes and you can be on your way."

Ralph took a seat on the medical stool covered with thin white paper. He watched the nurse as she gathered all her tools. She sat a basin beside Ralph, along with a pair of scissors, then put on some latex gloves. "Alright. If you'd lift your shirt, I can start removing these staples." One by one, the nurse plucked the staples inside the basin, using the scissors. "There we go. You didn't feel a thing, did you?" asked the nurse, as she plucked the last staple from Ralph's stomach. She cleaned around the wound, which ran down from Ralph's chest to his navel.
"Thank you" Ralph said.
"Oh, you're welcome. You just stay out of the line of fire. And make sure you clean the wound at least twice a day. Other than that, you should be just fine."

Ralph thanked the nurse again, then stepped out of the exam room back into the waiting area. He flipped his cell open and called Swift, as he walked out the sliding

hospital doors and into the parking lot. "Where ya'll at?" asked Ralph. "A'ight. I'm on my way, so don't leave."
Ralph climbed behind the wheel of his rental, a white 430 Lexus, and pulled out of the parking lot. He took Outer Drive straight through Gratiot Ave. and turned down Rosemary. Ralph could see Tuff, Robin and J-Nutty's three Chargers parked on the sidewalk and front lawn of the house. He parked across the street, then got out of the Lexus.
"My nigga!" J-Nutty said excited, as he rushed out the front door. He met Ralph on the walkway leading up to the steps.
"Check my war wounds. Check my war wounds. Every soldier got a story to tell," Tuff was singing the hook from one of Master P's songs. He was standing on the porch with his shirt off, jewelry everywhere. He had a blunt in one hand and a bottle of Moet in the other hand.
"This how ya'll do it," Ralph said, reaching for the Moet. 'Drink Mo' all day and blow blunts," he said, as if it was a question.
"Nah, for real this just my breakfast. I don't start drinkin' Crist until after two," laughed Tuff.
"Oh, shit. What up, my nigga?" Robin asked, stepping out of the house with Swift on his heels. You don't look shot, where you get hit at?" asked Robin.
Ralph turned and just looked at Swift. "You kow I can't hold water once I get that drank and DRO' in me" Swift said smiling.
"Yeah. You shoulda' seen this nigga. He broke down cryin' and everything last night while we was with some hoes. The hoes were laughing and shit" Tuff said.
"Let us see where you got hit at" Robin said excitedly.
Ralph pulled his shirt up. "Damn…" they all said in unison.
"I told the nigga, we should go back out there and body ole' boy. Nigga, got your stomach lookin' like a pot of chittlins" Swift laughed.

"And I told you that I wanted to forget about it. Other than ballin', what have ya'll been up to? How many heads have ya'll scratched of the list?" asked Ralph. They all dropped their heads. "Just like I thought."
"Nigga, we take one week off, and you act like we ain't handlin' business" Tuff pleaded.
"You haven't been handling B.I. I mean, it's cool to ball out, hit the club and stunt. Yeah, all that is cool, but let's not forget how we came into all this shit. J, do you think you'd be riding a brand new Charger if Pharaoh hadn't put us on?"
"Nah," answered J-Nutty.
"So, what do you think is going to happen if Pharaoh goes back to jail? It's back to rock bottom for all us. Back on some petty stick-up shit. Ain't nobody else gone open up no lane for us to eat like this. All I'm saying is let's not lose that killer instinct that got us here in the first place. We got one more nigga to find and kill. That bitch nigga, Tez," Ralph told them.
"Yo' what that nigga look like?" Everybody else on the list had an address, this nigga's just out there?" Robin asked.
"I'ma get a picture of the nigga from Pharaoh. I'm 'bout to go holla' at him right now. But put the word out there, that niggas is lookin' for his ass. And that we willin' to pay for the nigga's whereabouts" Ralph said, looking at his watch. "Look,' I'ma get up with ya'll later."
"A'ight, my nigga…" They all gave Ralph a play, then Swift walked him to his rental.
"I know yo' ass salty with me" Swift mumbled.
"I'll get over it. You know you're my mothafucka, I can't stay mad at you for too long," Ralph said, smiling. He threw a play jab at Swift's chest. "But nah, serious though. You 'bout done with the sack?" asked Ralph.
"Just 'bout. We'll sit down and fuck with the numbers in the morning.".

"A'ight. Keep an eye on them niggas. I know what I said went in one ear and out the other. I'm up," Ralph said. He gave Swift some dap, then climbed in the 430.

Ralph punched the Lexus down Gratiot Ave. He turned down Harper and took it down to Jefferson, where he drove to the Ambassador Bridge. Ralph flashed his phony license at the customs agent, and then crossed over the bridge into Windsor. Pharaoh's waterfront property was only about five minutes from the bridge. Ralph pulled into the driveway and honked his horn, then got out. Pharaoh wasn't answering the door, so Ralph walked around the side of the house. He could see Pharaoh perched on the boat sitting at the dock. Pharaoh smiled, then waved Ralph over.

"What up doe, old man," Ralph said, laughing as he approached the boat.

"Old man. Who you calling old, nigga?" Pharaoh stood up to let Ralph on the boat.

"Yo', look at you, out here drinking beer and fishing. Since when you start fishing?" Ralph asked, laughing.

"Shit, I'm just tryna' find a way to keep my sanity. I ain't caught nay fish since I've been out here, but something keeps eating my damn bait," Pharaoh said, pulling his fishing pole out of the water and looking at the hook. "Fuck it…" he said, then sat the pole down in the back of the boat. "So, what's up with you. You been too busy to come holla at the old man, huh?" asked Pharaoh.

"Nah. I had to take care of a few things, but nothing too major. Plus I wanted to have some good news for you when I came and saw you" Ralph said.

Pharaoh's eyes got big as he turned and faced Ralph. "What you got him" he asked.

"Not yet, but I'm on it. I need a picture of the nigga."

"Why, you know what Tez looks like, don't you?" asked Pharaoh.

"Yeah, I do. But I got my niggas on it too, more eye, feel me. Them niggas will body Tez on sight" Ralph explained.
"I got this one picture of us, and I want it back," Pharaoh said, as he dug into his wallet. He removed a picture of him, Tez and Ollie from one of the plastic inserts. He looked at it and smiled, then handed it to Ralph. "We was in Vegas right there. We had hit the Bellagio to see Roy Jones Jr. fight some bumb…" Pharaoh recalled that night's event, while Ralph looked down at the picture. "That's why I need that back so, guard it" Pharaoh ordered.
Ralph tucked the picture in his pants pocket, then reached in the cooler for a beer. He tried to lighten the mood, 'cause he could tell that Pharaoh was a bit distraught. Ralph cracked the top of his MGD, "I can't wait 'til I get old, so I can buy a boat and sit on the water tossing back brews."
"Here you go with this old shit," laughed Pharaoh. "Nigga, I still got it. Put 'em up" Pharaoh said, as he started shadow boxing. He threw an upper-cut to Ralph's stomach.
"Ah… shit," Ralph said in agony. Pharaoh had hit him dead on his wound.
"You good?" asked Pharaoh. He put his arm around Ralph, while he hunched over. I barely hit you."
Ralph gained his composure, then stood up. "Yeah, I'm cool," he said.
"Old. I'll show you old," laughed Pharaoh. Ralph smiled and played it off. They chilled out on the boat drinking beer just kicking it, 'til the sun went down.

Chapter Twenty-Two

"That's how you treat a real nigga, you give 'em the wrong number?" J-Nutty asked Chyna as she pulled up on their V.I.P. booth.

J-Nutty, Tuff, Robin and Swift were at 007 paying their huslta' taxes by making it rain. "I didn't give you the wrong number, it just wasn't my number" Chyna snapped.

"Ah, bitch. You got jokes, huh. Matter of fact, bitch get on skates. Send ole' girl over here to wait on us" J-Nutty said. He was waving the other bar maid over. Chyna was standing there with the shit face, she was trying to find something to say, but couldn't come up with anything, so she stormed off.

"That's right, you nothin' ass bitch. Beat it," laughed J-Nutty. He taunted Chyna, as she stormed towards the bathroom.

"Where you going lookin' so mean," Tez said, sticking his arm out from his booth. He grabbed Chyna by the waist and pulled her inside the booth.

"Get yo' funky hands off me, Tez," ordered Chyna.

"I don't know why you fighting it. You know I be all on your mind when you're at home at night. I beat this pussy up" Tez said, looking down between Chyna's legs.

"Let me up," Chyna pushed Tez's chest trying to free herself.

"Calm down. I'm just fuckin' with you. I stopped you because I wanted to ask you about those lil' niggas posted by the bar."

"Why you ain't ask yo' bitch?" asked Chyna. She nodded in Lil' One's direction who was giving Robin a lap dance.

"I knew you be watching a nigga. But anyway, I'm asking you. I know you keep your ear to the street, and I been

seeing how young dawg been at you. What's up with him?" asked Tez.
"My hand is itching," Chyna said, holding out her hand.
"You should try washing it, but here," Tez said, then stuffed a hundred dollar bill in Chyna's hand.
"All I know is that they call themselves the 7 Mile Dawgz and that they sell weed."
"Is that right?" Tez was eyeing all them niggas with one thing on his mind, murder. "How much weed we talkin', some petty shit, or some pounds?" asked Tez.
"I don't know, but the nigga right there with the Detroit Tiger's hat on, he gave me a couple of jars of that DRO' all these niggas in the city running around crazy for." Bingo! It hit Tez. These were the little niggas he heard about who had that good Hydro.
"I been watching you, you're right. And I've been seeing what you and that lil' bitch of yours been doing" Chyna said with an attitude.
"What are you talkin' 'bout?" asked Tez.
"Just know that all eyes aren't blind" Chyna said, as she slid out of the booth. "Thank you," she said, tucking the hundred in her bra.
"You leaving with me tonight?" asked Robin.
"Is you asking me, or tellin' me?" asked Lil' One. She was strapped to Robin's lap riding him to the beat of Freeway's 'Even though what we do is wrong.'
"I'm tellin' you" Robin said. He was buzzin' and geeked up from the lap dances.
"When you ready to go?" asked Lil' One.
"Shit, we can dip now."
"Just let me go change, and I'll be ready in a minute." Lil' One got up and walked toward the dressing room. She gave Tez the eye, like it was on.
'I'm 'bout to fuck the shit outta baby girl" Robin boasted to the crew.

"Look at you, hand-cuffin'. What's up with the bitch, you think she's on the house?" asked Swift.
"Nah, man."
"You know this lame-ass nigga ain't got no game. He don't know how to set a bitch out" Tuff said.
"I tell ya'll what. I'ma take the bitch back to the crib. I'ma smash, and then ya'll fall through and try ya' hand" Robin told them.
"A'ight. Here she comes" J-Nutty warned.
"You ready?" Lil' One asked, stopping in front of the booth.
"I'ma holla' at ya'll later," Robin said. He gave all of them some dap, then slid out of the booth.

Robin led the way out of club. The valet pulled his platinum Charger, sitting on 24's, up to the entrance. Lil' One jumped straight on Robin's dick. "This your car?" she asked, gushing like an official car-hopper. "Yeah," Robin answered, cheesin'. They got in the car and Robin stunted by flipping down the two visors revealing TVs. He reached in the backseat and flipped down the two 10" screens from the ceiling, then hit the Kenwood touch-screen. The four-twelves in the trunk came alive, as 50 Cent's 'Many Men' filled the car. Robin peeled out of the parking lot making a left on Outer Drive. Lil' One did what she does best; she unzipped Robin's shorts, then swallowed down on his limp dick. She found her rhythm as Robin rocked up in her mouth. As Robin turned the corner of Rosemary Street, Lil' One was putting the finishing touches on the pipe. It was like she took a screw out of her neck, the way her neck slid up and down she looked like a bobble head. She felt Robin's head expand in her mouth, so she sucked down and jacked the base of his dick, making him explode. "Ahh.." Robin sighed, as he pulled Lil' One's head up and down on his dick. "Hmm" moaned Lil' One. She pulled Robin's dick out of her mouth like it was a Blow Pop. Cum stuck to her tongue like honey as she raised her head up. She clipped the strand of nut with her index finger, then put it in her mouth. "That's what you call killer head" Lil' One said, smiling. "I can't argue with you on that one," Robin said. He pulled into the driveway of the house and parked. He pulled his pants up and got out of the car. Lil' One followed Robin up the stairs to the porch. He opened the door and let Lil' One in first.

"This is the crib," Robin said, waving his hand around the living room."

"You stay here by yourself?" asked Lil' One, as she took a seat on the sofa.

"Nah, me, my brother and my nigga J-Nutty. It's basically like our chill house. We just kick it and chill" Robin explained. He flopped down next to Lil' One and started breaking down a Swiser.

"So, what is it that you do for a living? Yo' ass is too young to be stuntin' as hard as you is."

"You see this," Robin said, handing Lil' One a jar of DRO. "That's what I do for a living," he said, then took the jar back from Lil' One. He twisted the cap open and dumped the weed inside the blunt.

"I know somebody who might be interested in buying some of that. How much for a pound of that?" asked Lil' One.

"Thirty-five hun'd. But I'll let you get 'em for three stacks" Robin said. He twisted the blunt into an L, then fanned it dry with his lighter. Robin sparked the L. He hit it twice, then passed it to Lil' One. She damn near threw up after hitting the blunt.

"Here take this, your tryna' kill a bitch," she said, coughing. Robin was laughing because he knew that was going to happen. He took a few more pulls off the blunt, then sat it in the ashtray.

"Take some of this off," Robin said, pulling at Lil' One's wife-beater. He helped her out of her shirt and started sucking on Lil' One's perfect C cup titties. Her

nipples were throbbing, as Robin inhaled them into his mouth. She leaned her head back and closed her eyes in ecstasy.
Robin worked his way up to Lil' Ones neck. He could feel steam rising from her, as he kissed around the sides of her neck. He slid his hands down to Lil' One's jeans and unbuttoned them. "Pull these off," he whispered. Robin undressed while he watched Lil' One peel out of her skin tight pants. She smelled like strawberry scented Bath & Body Works lotion, as she climbed on top of Robin's dick. He was so geeked up to be fucking such a bad little bitch, he didn't even think to put a condom on. Lil' One slid down on Robin's dick, while holding it at the base to guide him in. "Hahh.." she sighed taking all 8 inches. Robin gripped, Lil' One by the waist and slid her up and down on his dick to his satisfaction. She arched her back and dug her nails in Robin's chest, while she threw that pussy back on him. Feeling himself about to bust, Robin pulled out and rolled Lil' One over onto her knees. He had wanted to hit that ass from the back since the first time he saw her in the club. Robin palmed her ass cheeks, spreading them open so he could watch his dick slide inside a silk glove. Lil' One gritted her teeth as Robin began digging her guts out. She put her elbows down into the pillows of the sofa, and used them to rock back on. She met Robin's every thrust.

"Let's see what this lame got going," Tuff said, talking about Robin. Tuff turned the door knob to the front door, then stepped inside the house. "The lame doing big thangs" J-Nutty said, smiling. He was unfastening his pants a he walked into the living room. He sat on the sofa where Lil' One's head was. He stuck his dick smooth in Lil' One's mouth. She didn't refuse him. She began giving J-Nutty some of the 'killer head' she said she had. Robin bust off and got up. He was salty that Lil' One hadn't said anything. "That's right. Slide to the side, and let a real nigga drive" Tuff teased. He was already butt naked waiting to climb inside Lil' One. Tuff took Robin's spot on the sofa, and slid his hard dick right up in Lil' One from the back, while she gave J-Nutty head. Swift was standing in front of the sofa with his dick in his hand. He was waiting for Tuff or J-Nutty to get up. Whichever one bust first, that's whose place he was taking. They tossed Lil' One up all night. Robin's sucka simp ass was sick 'cause he wanted to try and make Lil' One his bitch, but he got over it after seeing her take all that pipe. They all fucked themselves to sleep and crashed out in the living room, on the sofa, and some on the floor.

Chapter Twenty-Three

The next morning, Robin drove Lil' One to her apartment. She told him that she wanted to introduce him to her brother, and that she was sure he would want to buy some DRO. Robin took two loose pounds, just in case Lil' One's brother wanted something right then.

"Damn, this is a nice spot," Robin said, as he pulled into the parking lot of Lakeside Apartment Complex. "How much you paying a month to be out here?" asked Robin.

"Not too much. Why, you tryna' help a bitch pay some bills?" asked Lil' One.

"Nah, you got it covered." Robin was still thinking about last night's demo.

Lil' One laughed 'cause she knew what he meant. "Boy, you's a mess. Pull over right here," she said directing Robin to her parking spaces. "Come on, he's home. That's his car right there" Lil' One said, nodding at Tez's Audi.

Robin looked at the car. He knew that car from somewhere, but couldn't place it. "Who's your brother?" asked Robin, as he followed Lil' One up the stairs to her complex.

"Oh, you've probably never heard of him. He's outta town most of the time. I be pushing his whips while he's gone." Lil' One lied. That put Robin at ease, because that's where he remembered seeing that Audi, outside 007. Lil' One led the way down the hall to her apartment. She stuck the key inside the door, then pushed it open.

"Tee, I'm home! I have company, somebody I want you to meet!" Lil' One yelled through the apartment.

Tez stepped out of the bedroom as Lil' One was walking down the hallway. She bucked her eyes as if to give Tez a signal, then jerked her head back toward the living room.

She switched up Tez's name so Robin wouldn't know his real name.
"Tee, I have someone I want you to meet. He's got something I know you'd be interested in. "Lil' One escorted Tez out to the living room where Robin stood.
"Robin, this is my brother, Tee. Robin has some DRO', and at a good price. I'ma let ya'll two talk. I'll be in the back if ya'll need me" Lil' One said. She stepped off, and let Robin and Tee get acquainted.
"What up doe," Tee said, extending his hand to give Robin a play.
"A'ight," Robin said.
Tez was lookin' Robin over. 'This that young nigga from the club. One of them 7 Mile Dawg niggas,' Tez told himself. "Have a seat man."
"Nah, I can't stay too long."
"A'ight then, let's see what you workin' with."
"I'll be right back. I left it in the car." Robin stepped in the hallway and went out to the car to grab the weed.
"Where'd he go?" Lil' One asked as she walked into the living room.
"He went out to his car" Tez said, as he leaned in to give Lil' One a kiss.
"You want me to get the plastic, baby?" asked Lil' One.
"Nah, I'ma do something today, that I've never done before in my entire life."
"What's that baby?"
Knock. Knock. "It's open" Tez said. Robin pushed the door open and stepped into the living room. He walked over to where Tez stood, leaning against the back of the sofa. Robin dug inside the Foot Locker bag and pulled a pound out, then handed it to Tez.
"This that funk" Tez said, as he opened the Ziploc bag and stuck his face down in the buds.

"Nah, that's that ew-wee" he laughed. He zipped the bag closed, then handed it back to Robin.
"How much you want for that," asked Tez.
"I told Lil' One, I'd let her get it for three G's."
"How many you got with you?"
"Two right now, but I can hook you up with as many as you need."
"A'ight, yeah. I'll take them two," Tez said, digging in his pants pocket. He pulled out a donkey knot, and started counting out six thousand dollars. "When can I get, say a hun'd pounds?" asked Tez.
"That's some light shit. I can have it for you just as soon as you count out three hun'd stacks."

Tez had to bite his tongue, which was something he never did. Robin was popping too slick out his mouth, he just didn't know that he was in the presence of Tez. "Here," Tez gave Robin the six G's for the two pounds. "And you're right, it is some light shit. I can have that money counted out in less than an hour. But I want those hun'd pounds."
"A'ight." Lil' One, I'ma fuck with you later. Hit me up," Robin said, before leaving out.
Lil' One locked the door behind him, then leaned against the door facing Tez. "What?" asked Tez. Lil' One had both of her hands on her face.
"I can't believe it. You actually paid for something. I just knew you were going to kill his ass, baby. Are you okay?" asked Lil' One.
"Very funny. Trust me it took everything I had not to kill his ass; especially when he started tryna' boss up on me. Did you see the lil' nigga?"
"Yeah. That's why I just knew you were going to give him the business,"

"Oh, I'ma give him the bizness. Right after he hand over those hun'd pounds. You think he's got that kind of work?" asked Tez.

"I think so. He and his lil' crew is gettin' money. They all ridin' good."

"A'ight. I want you to count out three hun'd thousand G's and put it in my suitcase. We gone see if lil' dawg can handle his bizness." He emptied one of the pounds into a fruit bowl, then sat it on the coffee table in the living room. Tez rolled up a blunt of DRO and kicked back, while Lil' One was in the bedroom counting out the money.

"7 Mile Dawgz. Bitch-ass niggas" Tez mumbled, as he exhaled smoke through his nose. He was plotting how he would stank all them niggas and take the weed.

Chapter Twenty-Four

"Where you know this nigga from?" asked Swift.
"The bitch we tossed up last night. It's her big brother" Robin explained. He took a seat on the edge of the sofa next to Swift, who was playing Tuff in *NBA Live '03* on Playstation II.
"What's his name?" asked Swift.
"Tee" Robin said.
"I don't know no, Tee. You know a, Tee?" Swift asked Tuff.
"Nope," Tuff said, not breaking his stare from the screen.
Robin dug in his pocket and slapped the six G's on the table that Tez just gave him. "The nigga is good money. He just bought two p's from me" Robin bragged.
"That's only two pounds. There's a big ass difference between two pounds and a hun'd. Like two hun'd and ninety thousand difference. I don't know, let me holla at Ralph to see if he knows the nigga" Swift said.
"Ya'll niggas don't know everybody in this city. You act like we been gettin' money for ten years," Robin said. He got frustrated and walked out the front room and out the door. He let the door slam, but Swift and Tuff hadn't heard it slam, they were caught up in their game.
"What up doe," Ralph said, he was getting out of his 430 Lex.

Robin was about to get in his car. "Ain't shit. 'Bout to go grab something to eat" he mumbled.
"A'ight. I'll be here, said Ralph, as he climbed the steps of the porch. He turned the knob on the door and stepped inside the house.
"What up doe," Ralph said, stepping into the living room.
"What it is?" said Swift.

"Ya'll niggas still playin' this shit. I don't see how ya'll do it. I can't sit in front of no TV for hours at a time" Ralph said, shaking his head.
"Hit some of this DRO, and you'll be glued right here beside us," Tuff said. "Here," he said, trying to pass Ralph the L.
"Man, you gone stop playin'," J-Nutty said, then rolled over and started snoring again.
"Pause the game for a second. I want to show ya'll something" Ralph said. Tuff and Swift hadn't heard Ralph's request. Ralph stood up and turned the TV off.
"Man, what the fuck you trippin' on now?" Swift ran around Ralph and turned the screen back on, then paused the game.
"I want ya'll to take a look at something," Ralph said, as he pulled the photo out of his pocket that Pharaoh had given him. He handed the picture to Swift. "That's Pharaoh, Ollie and Tez. That's Tez in the middle,"
"Yo' dawg looks familiar" Swift said. He was trying to jog his memory as to where he had seen Tez before.
"Let me see" Tuff said, taking the picture.
Swift passed him the picture, and Tuff zoomed in on Tez.
"That's ole' boy who be up in 007" Tuff yelled.
"You sure?" Ralph asked excited.
"Yeah, the nigga be tucked in the booth by the bathroom, laying low like a mothafucka can't see him back there. Matter of fact, he was in there last night. The nigga got the new Audi on blades" Tuff said.
"How many times have you seen him in there?" asked Ralph.
"Shit, every night" Tuff replied.
"I'm tryna' see who you're talkin' 'bout" Swift said.
"You ain't gone know. Yo' ass be in there slippin'. If it wasn't for me, a nigga woulda' jacked all ya'll asses. I be on point" Tuff bragged.

Ralph had stepped into the dining room and called Pharaoh. "I'm positive. They say he's in there every night" Ralph told him. Pharaoh knew that was his Tez. Tez used to live in 007 back when they was eating. 'That nigga must of hit a lick,' Pharaoh thought.
"A'ight, well you know what to do. Ralph, give me a call soon as it's done."

Pharoah hung up his cell phone, then smiled. Pharaoh looked over at the skyline of downtown Detroit. He was sitting out in the water in his cigar boat. "I knew you couldn't sit still for too long. That ass is 'bout to be mines" Pharaoh said loudly. He rejoiced in the fact that it wouldn't be long before he could enact phase two of his master plan, so he could go back to living his life. He cracked a fresh MGD, then raised his can to the sky. "Here's to you," he said, talking to Tez.

Chapter Twenty-Five

"Hello," answered Robin.
"Where you at?" asked Lil' One.
"I'm around." Robin had just pulled out of the parking lot of Coney Island on Gratiot Ave. and Outer Drive.
"My brother wants to know what time you wanna hook up?" asked Lil' One.
"He got the bread don't he?"
"Nigga, I wouldn't be callin' you if he didn't. Can you handle the order is the question?"
Robin didn't want to reveal that he had to go through Ralph and Swift, so he locked it in. "Yeah, I can handle it. Look, I'ma call you back in 'bout twenty minutes, and let you know where to meet me at."
"A'ight. In a minute." *Click.*
"What he say?" asked Tez. He was suiting up in all black and loading his trusted 40 cal. That gun had to have at least a hundred bodies on it.
"He's going to call me back and let me know where to meet him at" Lil' One said.
"That's where he's going to die at, too" Tez said with a stone-cold look on his face. He was getting pumped, just thinking about it made his dick hard.

Robin pulled into the driveway of the crib on Rosemary. He grabbed his food out of the passenger seat, then got out of the car. He climbed the steps to the porch and turned the knob, opening the front door. He looked around the front room, Tuff and Swift were gone. He tapped J-Nutty who was still asleep on the sofa. "Get the fuck off me," J-Nutty said, without rolling over to see who it was tapping him. Within seconds, he was back to a deep sleep, snoring.

Robin looked out the front window, Tuff and Swift's cars were still out there, but then Robin remembered that Ralph had pulled up when he was leaving. 'They probably left with Ralph,' Robin told himself. He walked into the back porch of the house and opened the deep freezer where Swift kept the DRO. Robin counted out a hundred pounds, then closed the freezer door. He stuffed the pounds into grocery bags, two in each bag, then carried the bag outside and put them in his trunk. Robin climbed in his car and backed out. He was going to show Swift that he could hold his own and push weight just like he and Ralph. He flipped open his cell phone and called Lil' One's cell.
"This him right here…hello," answered Lil' One.
"Yeah, tell yo' brother I said to meet me…"
"Nah, listen young dawg. You gone meet me at the Sueze Motel on 8 Mile and Ryan," Tez said, snatching the phone from Lil' One.
"I'm on my way." Robin put his seatbelt on and sat his seat up. He drove with both hands on the steering wheel, and played the rear-view mirror.

*****

It was still early in the day, but Ralph was itching to kill Tez. He, Tuff and Swift all piled into the Lex and went up to 007. "His car be parked right there every night" Tuff said, pointing to an empty parking space in front of the club. Ralph valet parked the 430, then they all stepped off in the club. It was only one something in the afternoon, so the club was bare, with the exception of a few old men gawking at the two dancers performing their set. Ralph, Tuff and Swift took a seat near the stage. Ralph wanted to be as close to the door as possible in case Tez came in the club, they'd have him boxed in.

"Can I help you?" Chyna asked, as she pulled up on their table.
"Bitch, is you stupid or dumb?" asked Tuff. "We ain't fuckin' with you after how you tried to shit on my man" Tuff said, on behalf of J-Nutty.
"Chill out" Ralph said, not knowing what was going on. "Let me get a bottle of Crist and whatever else my niggas want" he told Chyna.
"And you?" asked Chyna. She stood with her pad and pen ready to take Tuff and Swift's order.
"Just bring us three bottles of Crist" Swift snapped.
"What's up with her?" asked Ralph, as Chyna walked away to go fill their orders.
"Ah, J-Nutty was tryna' holla at her, but she got on some bullshit like niggas was peon's or something" Swift explained.
"Word… where you say that bitch-nigga be sitting at?" asked Ralph.
"He be in that booth right there," Tuff said, nodding toward the back of the club, where an empty booth sat.
"Here ya'll go," Chyna sat the three bottles on the table, then popped the corks. She stood by waiting on her tip.
"Oh, my bad." Ralph dug in his pocket and gave Chyna two twenties.
"Thank you" Chyna said. She rolled her eyes at Tuff, then spun on her heels. Ralph grabbed her by the hand before she could walk away.
"What?" Chyna snapped. She thought that Ralph was about to try and holla at her.
"Let me ask you something." "Your in here every night?" Ralph asked.
"Five nights, some times six, why?" asked Chyna.
"You know him?" asked Ralph, as he tried to hand Chyna the photo.

"What are you, a detective or something?" asked Chyna, refusing to take the photo.
"Oh, my bad…" said Ralph. He dug in his pocket again and handed Chyna a hundred dollar bill this time.
Chyna snatched the photo from Ralph. "It's the one in the middle I'm interested in."
Chyna looked at the picture and her eyes widened. "Where'd you…" she caught herself, then said, "What do you want to know?"
"I want to know his name, where he lives, what kind of car he drives, and what he orders every night from that booth over there," Ralph said, nodding in the direction of Tez's booth.
"All I know is his name, they call him Tez. He's in here every night. He be stalking niggas far as I'm concerned."
"What you mean stalking?"
"He be watching niggas who be in here stuntin', then he'll sick this little stripper bitch on the nigga. She'll leave with the balla', and that'll be the last time I see him. A lot of niggas been comin' up missin', and they all was last seen with that lil' bitch,"
"Who is she talkin' 'bout?" Ralph asked Swift.
"You talkin' 'bout ole' girl that calls herself Lil' One?" Swift asked Chyna.
"Yeah, that's her. I think she's Tez's girlfriend. But I know that something ain't right with them, and as a matter of fact, he was asking about ya'll last night…" said Chyna.
"Fuck he asking 'bout us for?" Where that bitch nigga at? I'ma stank his ass on sight!" said J-Nutty. He was getting hyped.
"Calm down, Jay. A'ight, thank you baby girl" Ralph said.
"Can I keep this?" asked Chyna, talking about the photo.
"Why?" asked Ralph.
"I have my reasons."

"I can't. I told the person who gave it to me, I'd return it." Chyna wondered if he was talking about Pharaoh. She reluctantly gave Ralph back the photo, then walked away.
"A, that's the bitch we had at the crib last night" Swift said.
"Who?" asked Ralph.
"Lil' One. Tez's girlfriend" Swift revealed.
"Word." Ralph eyes widened.
"Yeah. But get this. Robin told me that the bitch's brother, some nigga name, Tee wanted to snatch a hun'd elbows. He bought two from Robin. But I told the nigga I was gone holla' at you to see if you knew him. You think Tee is Tez?" asked Swift.
Tuff was already walking out the door. He had his cell phone to his ear. "Come on baby bro, pick up the phone," Tuff mumbled.

*****

Robin had just gotten out of the car and was walking up to the room door where Tez was standing. They were at the Suez Motel on 8 Mile and Ryan. "What up doe" Tez said, extending his hand for a play. He and Robin stepped inside the hotel room Tez had Lil' One rent. She was sitting on the bed pretending to be counting money when Robin stepped in the room. Tez looked around the parking lot then closed the door and locked it.
"You got the work with you?" asked Tez, as he stepped into the room behind Robin.
"Yeah, it's in the trunk" Robin answered.
"Good, this won't take long at all." Tez walked over to the bed and dug inside his suitcase. He pulled out his trusted 40 cal. and raised it to Robin's chest. He waited for that dose of medicine called fear to set in. Robin's eyes bucked at the sight of the gun. "Who's following you?" asked Tez.
"Nobody. I swear" Robin stuttered.
"Who did you tell you were meeting me here?"
"Nobody…" said Robin, sounding like he was about to cry.

"Stupid mothafucka." *Boom! Boom! Boom!*

Tez dropped Robin where he stood. Robin's body slumped down to the floor. Blood was seeping out of the bullet holes in his chest and onto the plastic Lil' One had laid out just before Robin pulled up. Tez, stood over Robin and pumped two more slugs into his head. *Boom! Boom!* "You shoulda at least lied, you stupid young mothafucka," he said, talking to Robin's dead body. "Baby, roll this bitch up, while I pull the car up," ordered Tez. He stepped outside of the room. Lil' One zipped the suitcase shut and sat it by the door, then did as Tez told her. She rolled Robin up tightly in the plastic, then rolled him into the comforter off the bed.

"You ready?" Tez asked, stepping back inside the room.

"Yeah. Help me lift this bitch" Lil' One grunted. Tez and Lil' One carried Robin outside and put him in the trunk of Tez's Audi.

"I'ma take his car and get the weed out," Tez said. He gave Lil' One a kiss, then jumped in Robin's Charger. He skirted out of the parking lot and turned onto 8 Mile Road heading west.

Ring... Ring... Ring... Tez looked around, then pulled Robin's cell phone out from the console. *Ring... Ring..* "Hello," answered Tez.

"Robin, where are you?" asked Tuff.

"Robin is no longer with us" Tez said coldly. He rolled down the window and chunked the cell phone into traffic.

"Hello… Hello!" yelled Tuff.

"What happend!" asked Swift, from the passenger seat of Ralph's 430 Lex. They were on their way back to the house.

"That nigga got Robin." Tuff yelled.

"What?" asked Ralph, turning in his seat to face Tuff. "Who was that on the phone?" he asked.

"Some nigga, talkin' 'bout, Robin is no longer with us…"

"We gone find him," assured Swift.
"You that's all I got, baby bro" said Tuff. He was devastated. His hurt was quickly turning into anger.

Ralph came to a screeching stop in front of the house on Rosemary. They all jumped out the car and ran inside the house. The noise startled J-Nutty, who was still asleep. He jumped up at the sound of the screen door slamming hard against the brick wall of the porch.
"Where's Robin?" Ralph asked J-Nutty.
"I don't know, I been sleep" J-Nutty mumbled.
Swift rushed to the back porch. He went straight for the deep freezer. "Please don't let nothin' be missin'" Swift said, as he raised the lid to the freezer. He could tell from the way the pounds were situated that someone had been in there. "Damn…" sighed Swift.
"What's up, did he take anything?" asked Ralph, stepping onto the back porch.
"Yeah. That nigga went to meet with Tez. I told that nigga to hold up." Swift slammed the freezer shut. He wasn't tripping about the hundred pounds, he was mad that Robin hadn't listened to him, and now he was missing.
"You think he killed him?" asked Ralph.
"I hope not," Swift said softly.
As they walked back into the front room, Tuff was peeling out the driveway. Ralph ran to the front door, but it was too late, Tuff was bending the corner onto Gratiot Ave.
"Come on, let's catch this nigga before he does something crazy" Ralph said

Chapter Twenty-Six

Tez dropped the weed off at his apartment, then met Lil' One at Broadway junkyard on Mound Road and Six Mile.

"What took you so long? I was starting to get worried" Lil' One said, as Tez climbed inside the passenger seat of his Audi.

"You know better than to be worrying." Tez leaned over and gave Lil' One a kiss. "Now, pull into the yard," directed Tez.

Lil' One inched the wide-body Audi through the narrow fence into the junkyard. "Pull over there behind that Crown Vic," Tez said, while pointing to a black, battered Crown Victoria.

Lil' One parked the car, and they both got out. Tez walked around the passenger side of the Crown Vic, and opened the door. He reached inside and opened the glove box. He pushed the trunk button and the trunk flew open. He walked around the back of the car and lifted the trunk on the Audi. "Come on, baby. Help me with him." Tez. Tez grabbed Robin's feet, and together He and Lil' One slung Robin's feet inside the trunk of the Crown Vic. Tez closed the trunk and dusted himself clean. He banged his fist on the trunk of the Crown Vic, and said "I'll holla…" He and Lil' One jumped back in the Audi and peeled out. Tez left Robin's Charger parked across the street from Broadway.

"What about his boys?" asked Lil' One, as she turned down Mt. Elliot.

"Oh, they're next. Greed is a mothafucka. They'll be sitting in a trunk next to their man soon."

"No, I mean. What do you think they're going to do? You really don't think he told nobody he was going to meet you, and that you were my brother?" asked Lil' One. She was a little bit nervous. She saw how the 7 Mile Dawgz got down.

"Nah, I don't think so. You heard the lil' nigga. That's why I asked him that 'cause if he would of said yeah, then I would've held him until I could kill the other ones. But now they're just sittin' ducks. And besides, bitch I'm me. Not a nigga in this city wants it with Tez," he said, waving his 40 cal.

"I know, baby." Lil' One said, smiling.

"Then act like you know. When you didn't come home the other night you went to the lil' nigga's crib, didn't you?"

"Yeah."

"A'ight, show me where it's at. I know they gotta have some money in there 'cause I ain't 'bout to be out here sellin' no weed, I'ma smoke all that."

*****

Tuff had one thing on his mind, murder! In his heart, he could feel that Robin was dead, but he had to know for certain, and kill whoever was responsible, in this case, Tez and Lil' One. Tuff pulled into the valet of 007 and jumped out, leaving the car running. He walked through the entrance and snatched the door open to the club. The bouncer recognized his face, so he didn't bother getting up to frisk Tuff. Tuff scanned the club from the doorway, and locked eyes on Chyna. He rushed over to the bar where Chyna was standing with her back to him. Tuff grabbed Chyna by the shoulder and jerked her around wildly.

"Nigga, get yo' fuckin' hands off me!" yelled Chyna.

"Where is she?" demanded Tuff.

"Where is who?" asked Chyna, all stankish. She had her face balled up, and was clutching the neck of a Corona bottle just in case Tuff grabbed her again.

"Lil' One. That bitch, and that nigga Tez?" asked Tuff.

"I don't know them like that," Chyna said, then tried to turn away.

"Bitch, you gone stop playin' games," Tuff said. He reached to grab Chyna's arm, but she bust the Corona over the top of his head.
"I got your bitch!" yelled Chyna, as she looked down at the floor where Tuff was. He was a little dazed, but his anger got him to his feet.
"You bitch…" Tuff said, stumbling. He squared off with Chyna.

She kicked her shoes off and put up her hands. "Bitch-nigga, come on," she said, rocking back and forth. Tuff cocked back and threw a wild punch, but missed Chyna by inches. The bouncer tackled Tuff from behind, and tried to restrain him. Ralph and Swift came running through the door. Ralph raced over to the scuffle and pulled the bouncer off of Tuff. "We got him, big dawg" Ralph said, pulling the bouncer back. Swift, was holding Tuff back.
"You wanna hit a woman, but you can't do shit with another man. You got yo' ass wooped" Chyna said, laughing.
"Bitch, fuck you!" yelled Tuff.

Swift, started dragging Tuff toward the front door. "I'ma K this bitch up!" yelled Tuff on his way out the door. The Arab owner, Ali, was standing behind the bar with a chrome AK-47 at his side. "I apologize Ali, I'll keep him outa here for a while" Ralph said. Ali, didn't say anything. He just nodded towards the door, like *leave*. Ralph exited the club to find Tuff out in the parking lot going nuts. "Ima K this bitch up! I'ma kill all you mothafuckas!" vowed Tuff. He was pacing back and forth, while looking at the club. Ralph tried to hug Tuff, but he pushed him away. "Fuck a hug. A hug ain't gone bring my lil' brother back. I done let this bitch ass nigga kill my baby brother," Tuff said, breaking down in tears. Ralph and Swift shared in Tuff's emotion. Robin was like a brother to all of them. They had been together since the start. Ralph couldn't help but blame himself, and the rest of them for Robin's death.

'If we would've found that nigga, and killed him, we wouldn't be going through this,' Ralph told himself, as he dropped a lone tear of hate.

Chapter Twenty-Seven

Ralph, Swift and Tuff went back to the house on Rosemary. They all sat silently in the living room, while Ralph paced the floor. He was trying to put a plan together. He knew that they had to catch Tez before he struck again. Do ya'll realize what has happened?" asked Ralph. He didn't wait for a response, he kept talking… "We have allowed a nigga who we were suppose to be looking for, we allowed him to kill one of us. Without a doubt, that bitch-nigga knows who all of us are. We gotta find that nigga. I know Tez, and he's nothin' to sleep on."

"So, what we gone do?" asked Swift.

"That ain't even the issue, 'cause we gone body the bitch-nigga. But finding him is the hard part" Ralph said.

"I say we hog-tie the owner until he tells us that lil' bitch's address" J-Nutty said with hate in his eyes.

"Nah, I got a better idea. I'ma find out where the nigga momma stay at. I'ma go holla at Pharaoh. Don't nobody do shit until I get back. We can't let him catch us slippin'," said Ralph. He grabbed his car keys off the flatscreen and took a look at Tuff who was sitting on the sofa.

"Take care of Tuff," Ralph told, Swift and J-Nutty, before stepping out the front door.

"That nigga think I'm 'bout to sit and wait on a call from O.G. Pharaoh, he crazy," Tuff said. He stood up and pulled the AR-15 and box of 223 shells from under the pillow of the sofa. Tuff began stuffing shells into the 30-round clip, using his shirt. "Load 'em clean. Empty clean," he said.

"Tuff, maybe we should wait on Ralph to get back. We gone get the nigga" Swift said, trying to talk some sense into Tuff.

"You can wait on that nigga. That's my lil' brother out there" Tuff yelled, as he continued to fill the clip.

*****

Ralph stomped the Lexus through downtown Detroit, and was pulling off the bridge into Canada. He flipped open his cell phone and dialed Pharoah's number. "I'm pulling up, come open the door." He threw his cell phone on the dashboard, then pulled into the driveway of Pharaoh's waterfront estate.

"Who was that?" asked Stacy. She and Pharaoh were laid up in the master bedroom. They'd been fuckin' all afternoon.

Pharaoh pulled the satin sheet off his naked body, then rolled out of bed. "That's my son" Pharaoh said, as he slid into his slippers and housecoat.

"Your son?" asked Stacy.

Ding- Dong! Ding- Dong! Ralph was pushing the doorbell.

"Relax. It's my play son." Pharaoh kissed Stacy, then hit the stairs.

Ding- Dong! Ding- Dong! Ralph was laying on the doorbell again. Pharaoh snatched the door open. He looked at Ralph, then over his shoulder.

"Somebody chasin' you?" asked Pharaoh. Ralph, pushed passed Pharaoh and walked into the kitchen.

"Okay…" said Pharaoh. He closed the front door and followed Ralph into the kitchen. "You mind tellin' me what's going on, the way you stormed in here, makes me think somebody got killed."

Ralph was pacing back and forth. "He killed my man, Robin."

"Who?" asked Pharaoh.

"Tez. He fuckin' killed my nigga."

Pharaoh was thrown for a whirl. His heart started racing. "Come out here" Pharaoh said, as he slid the back patio

door open. He didn't want Stacy to hear what they were talking about. "What happened?" he asked, closing the patio door.
"Tez, talked Robin into sellin' him some weed, and when he went to take it to him, Tez killed him."
"Who else was with Robin when he met up with Tez?"
"He went by his self…"
"Why would ya'll be sellin' Tez weed? Ya'll were 'pose to be tryna' kill his ass."
"We didn't know it was Tez. Some chick from 007 set Robin up. She told him that her brother wanted to buy some weed and that his name was Tee. Robin sold Tez two pounds. But Tez said he wanted another hun'd pounds. Robin asked Swift about it, and Swift told him to fall back on it until I green-lighted the shit. But I was over here with you at the time."
"So, let me guess. Robin took it upon himself to go meet with Tez all by himself, thinking it was some chick's brother, named Tee? And he took a hun'd pounds?" asked Pharaoh.
"Yeah…"
"Okay, so how do ya'll know he's dead, if nobody was with him?"
"Because when Tuff called Robin's cell, Tez picked up and said some slick shit like, 'he's no longer with us'…"
"This shit is crazy." Pharaoh looked over at the city. "So, I guess you want me to fix this?" he asked Ralph.
"Nah, I can handle it. I came to holla at you because I want to know where the nigga's momma stay at."
"I can't cross that line. Ms. Nance ain't got nothin' to do with this. This shit is between me and Tez."
"No it's not. It's between all us now. He done killed one of my brothers. It's all fair game now" Ralph yelled.
Pharaoh turned and looked at Ralph. "I want you to listen to me. Not a hair on Ms. Nance's head is going to be

touched. You got that?" He was staring into Ralph's eyes waiting on an answer. Lil' nigga, did you hear what I said?" asked Pharaoh.

Ralph looked away and clinched his jaw. "Yeah."

"Look, I know that was your man, but there's just certain things in life we don't do. I want Tez's head, too. Ain't a nigga who wants him dead more than me. I see the nigga in my sleep! But I won't allow anything to happen to the nigga's old bird, not comin' from me anyway…"

"Robin's blood is on my hand. And my niggas need answers."

"You tell them niggas exactly what I just told you. Ralph, you've got to realize where I'm comin' from, as I'm realizing where ya'll standing. And don't take this the wrong way, but not one of ya'll have a mother who's been there for ya'll, so ya'll don't understand that love. Tez's mom is basically like my mom. She helped raise me, too. I need you to understand that. I feel you because the only family you got is your niggas. But I'd like to think of us as family, too. I just got done tellin' my bitch that you were my son. Nigga, I mean that shit! I got nothin' but love for you. We are family; blood can't make us no closer. So, I'm asking you for me, not to cross that line. You got that, Ralph!" Pharaoh said, hugging him. "We gone get the nigga. I never said it was going to be easy. But we'll get him. I promise," Pharaoh held Ralph to his chest like a son. He was trying to show Ralph that he really did have love for him, and that it wasn't just about him needing Ralph to take care of the hit list. "I need you to believe me when I tell you, that if I were to get caught and go to jail for the rest of my life, I would still have the same love for you…" said Pharaoh. "Do you believe that?"

"Yeah." Ralph did. He knew Pharaoh kept it one hun'd all the way around the board.

"That's all that matters because knowing so will keep us loyal to one another." Pharaoh said.

Chapter Twenty-Eight

"Baby, I'm about to leave for work. You need me to do anything, before I go?" Lil' One was in the bathroom putting her earrings on. She checked her pretty one last time in the mirror, then slipped into the bedroom. Tez, was rolling up a bunch of blunts from the hydro he took from Robin.

"You hear me, baby. Do you need me to do anything before I leave?"

Tez, licked the seal of the blunt, then rolled it. "I'ma have you doing a whole lot tonight when you get home, so don't tire yourself out at work. We getting a room at the Four Seasons in Bloomfield tonight," Tez put the L to the side with the rest of the rolled blunts.

"Aww succy, succy. We gone get massages and order room service, baby?" Lil' One plopped down on the bed next to Tez.

"We gone do it big. All that fat-boy shit. Give me a kiss for you go."

Lil' One leaned over and gave Tez a wet, passionate kiss. "I love you, Tez," she said, looking him in his eyes.

"I love you too, boo Tez.

Lil' One kissed Tez once more, then rolled off the bed. She grabbed her purse and Tez's car keys and was out the door. She turned the radio on, and popped Eve's latest LP in. She skipped tracks to her favorite song. 'What ya'll niggas want. You can't touch. What ya'll niggas need..' Lil' One sang along to the chorus. She cracked the sunroof and raised her seat, so that she could be seen as she crossed 8 Mile into Detroit. Her hair was blowing in the wind, and she looked like a real life superstar with her bubble-eyed 'Cartier' wire frames, with the slight 30% pink tint. You

can't tell Lil' One nothing, she was on cloud nine. Back at home she had a nigga who was down for her crown, and didn't mind her being her. She had money, fine jewelry and pushin' a $150,000 machine through the city.
"I'ma boss-bitch," she said smiling to herself in the rear-view mirror, as she bent the corner of 7 Mile and Outer Drive.

Tuff was ducked low in his triple black Charger with tinted windows. He was parked across the street from 007 in front of the Alterwood Apartment building. His dick stood up at the sight of Tez's Audi blinging as it approached the parking entrance of 007. Tuff gripped the stock of his AR-15, letting his finger rest against its trigger. 'Damn', he thought as Lil' One pulled into the entrance. He was mad because Tez wasn't in the car with her. "Fuck it," Tuff said. He yanked the driver's side door open and tucked the AR behind his back as he waited for the oncoming traffic to clear.

The valet greeted Lil' One as she came to a stop in front of the valet shed. She slapped the car in park, then popped the trunk. "How you?" she asked the valet, as she walked around to the trunk. She reached down to grab her mini-suitcase she used to tote her dance clothes. She pulled her handle and lifted the case out of the trunk. She sat it on the ground and dug in her purse to tip the valet. Tuff broke into a spring while taking aim at the valet's chest. As soon as the valet looked up, Tuff put four 223's in his chest. *Laaka! Laaka! Laaka! Laaka!* The valet fell to his back, and Tuff focused his attention on Lil' One, who was digging in her purse. She had the handle of her chrome 380 with the pearl white pistol grip halfway out of her purse, when Tuff butted her in the side of the head with his AR-15. Tuff raced for Lil' One's pistol, which skidded across the parking lot, stopping at the entrance.

Lil' One tried to jump back in the car, but Tuff climbed in through the passenger seat. He put the gun to Lil' One's head. "Bitch, don't make me kill yo' ass, too."

"What do you want? Why are you doing this?" asked Lil' One.

"We ain't gone play these cat and mouse games. Bitch, I'ma ask you one time. Where is my brother?" Tuff cocked the hammer back on Lil' One's 380.

Lil' One could see the seriousness in Tuff's eyes and knew that she better not play any games. "He's at the house with my boyfriend. They're countin' out the money for the weed he sold him." Lil' One was trying to give Tuff some hope that Robin was still alive, maybe he wouldn't kill her, she thought.

"Back out and take me to them," ordered Tuff. He held Lil' One at gunpoint while she drove down Outer Drive. He held the gun low against the console, pointed at her side.

"Listen, bitch. I know Tez is your boyfriend. And I know that ya'll been settin' niggas up, and killin' them. I swear to God. Bitch, you betta pray that my brother is alive."

"You want me to call, so you can talk to him?" asked Lil' One. She was trying to figure out a way she could put Tez on game that she and Tuff were on their way to the apartment.

"Yeah. Get him on the phone," ordered Tuff.

Lil' One unplugged her cell phone from the cigarette charger and dialed the apartment number slowly, while she used her thumb to lower the volume. She pushed send, then pressed the phone to her ear as tight as she could. "Hello," answered Tez. "Hello… Baby, you there?" asked Tez. "Hello." Lil' One purposely waited a few moments before she said anything. She looked over at Tuff, then said "I got the answering machine they must be playin' that damn game or something." "Hello… Baby?" asked Tez. "Tez, it's me, baby. I'm on my way back home, if Robin is still there

have him call his brother because he's worried. He hasn't heard from him all day. Love you. Bye." Lil' One hung up the phone.
"Bitch, you betta hope he's there. Who the fuck answered Robin's phone earlier?" asked Tuff.
"Shit, I don't know. I'm tellin' you everything is straight, damn. You'll see" said Lil' One.
She and Tuff were both hoping so. Tuff was holding on to the thread of hope that Robin was still alive. And Lil' One was hoping her little message put Tez on point.

Tez was on point alright. He stuffed the blunt he'd been smoking into the ashtray, then jumped up from the sofa. "Yeah. It's war time" Tez said excited. He rubbed his hands together as he walked through the kitchen and down the hall to the bedroom. He stepped in the closet and pulled out his suitcase full of guns, toys as he called them. He settled on a 9 mm Ruger with an extended 30-round clip. "You should do the job," he said, holding the nine milly up for further inspection. He reached in his case of toys and pulled out a silencer, then screwed it onto the nose of the gun. He cocked the gun back, sliding one gold-plated shell into the chamber, then stuffed the case back inside the closet. Tez walked over to the dresser and removed his blue bullet-proof vest from the top drawer. He strapped into the vest and walked out of the bedroom back into the living room. Tez, knew that he had to get the up's on then, assuming that there was more than one. "You lil' bastards want it with me? I'ma show all ya'll why niggas fear the air I breathe." Tez opened the door to the apartment and stepped out into the hallway. He pulled the door shut, then walked to the end of the hall. He peeked out the window of the entry door into the parking lot. He didn't see any sign of Lil' One or anyone else. Tez opened the door next to the entrance of the complex, it was a maintenance room. He stepped inside the room and turned the lights out. He kneeled down and brought the door to a slight crack. From the crack he could see the cement landing of the entrance. He sat there and waited.

*****

"Bitch, where is Robin's car? I don't see his car." Tuff was scanning the parking lot of Lil' One's apartment complex.

"I don't know where he left his car. Tez picked Robin up somewhere and brought him out here so they could count the money." Lil' One was also scanning the lot for any signs of Tez. She pulled into her parking space, then hit her horn.

"What the fuck you think you're doin'? Tuff snapped.

"My bad, it's a habit" Lil' One said, as she cut the engine.

"Come on, and don't try nothin' slick, or I'ma bury yo' ass." Tuff took the car keys from Lil' One, then waved the pistol at her for her to get out.

Tuff got out of the car behind Lil' One, and tailed her up the stairs. He had the gun tucked in the side pocket of his Polo jacket, with it pointed dead on Lil' One's backpiece. They reached the top step and Tez saw Lil' One's shadow largening against the landing. He cocked the hammer back on his nine milly, and pulled the door shut, but held the knob so that the latch wouldn't catch.

"I'm tellin' you he's okay. I don't see why..."

"Shut the fuck up, and keep walking," Tuff waved his pocket at the entrance door. Lil' One took a deep breath, then pulled the door open.

Tez waited until he saw both pair of footsteps pass from under the door, then he slid out of the closet and put the silencer to the back of Tuff's dome. "Nigga, you bet not," Tez said through clenched teeth, as Tuff went to pull the gun out of his coat pocket.

"I think that belongs to me." Lil' One snatched her 380 from Tuff, then kissed Tez.

"Where the fuck is my brother at?" demanded Tuff.

"Nigga, you don't see this? This is a gun, lil' nigga. You ain't in no position to be making no damn demands. Bring yo' bitch ass on," ordered Tez. He shoved Tuff in the back, and tried to push him forward. Tuff wasn't going for it, though. He spun around and took a wild swing at Tez, but missed. His punch struck Lil' One in the side of her face. Tuff, tried charging past Tez, but the impact of two hot slugs sent him falling back.

"That's right, nigga. Fight back. I likes that. But I'm still gone body yo' young ass. Help me drag this bitch back to the closet Tez.

Tuff was dazed, but not out of it. He was hit twice in the stomach and was starting to leak pretty badly. "You bitch-ass nigga, you think you're going to get away with this. My niggas is gone kill yo' ass," Tuff said, as Tez and Lil' One dragged him inside the maintenance closet.

Lil' One shut the door behind them. Tez took the butt of his gun and started pistol whipping Tuff. "I told yo' ass. You – not- in no- position to be – talkin' – shit!" yelled Tez, as he emphasized his point with each blow. Tuff was bloody as E-mothafucka, and a little delirious, but he was still mumbling shit. That's why they called him Tuff, 'cause he never backed down from anything, not even death.

"Nigga. Fuc… Fuck you… bitch ass nigga. Pharaoh…" Tuff was blanking in and out.

"Pharaoh?" repeated Tez. He kneeled down and grabbed Tuff's face. "What about Pharaoh?" Tez demanded.

"He gone kill you," Tuff said, then blacked out. Tez, stood up and pumped two more slugs into Tuff's dome.

"Who is Pharaoh, baby?" quizzed Lil' One.

"A dead man" Tez replied. He was wondering what connection Tuff had to Pharaoh.

Chapter Twenty-Nine

J-Nutty was leaning over the glass dining room table, scooping DRO' into his awaiting blunt paper. "How I'm gone tell a grown man he can't leave? The nigga rolled out," J-Nutty said, talking about Tuff.

"You know Tuff ain't in his right mind," Swift said, following J-Nutty into the living room. They both took a seat on the sofa.

"If it were me, I'd be out there lookin' for my lil' brother, too. Shit, I tried to go with him, but Tuff said he wanted to go alone. I had to respect that." J-Nutty sparked the L, hit it two times, then tried to pass it to Swift.

"I'm good," Swift waved his hand, declining. "I can't even take an hour nap without one of ya'll comin' up missin." Swift picked up the cordless phone off the coffee table and dialed Tuff's cell number. The phone just rang repeatedly. Now he's not answering his phone."

"Ain't nothin' to talk about. You know Tuff, he's a'ight. That nigga's a warrior," J-Nutty said, in between pulls.

"Yeah. But this nigga, Tez is a beast." Swift hung up the phone and looked at the clock on the wall.

"Ralph didn't call, did he?"

"Nah. He still over there playin' house with that nigga Pharaoh. For real, I'm gettin' tired of all this flunkie shit. Here it is we gettin' late on the strength of this nigga's beef" J-Nutty said with an attitude.

"Jay, you trippin'. P, ain't been nothin' but good to us." All the money he has, he could've hired the best head hitters in the city to handle that list. But he gave us a shot and put us on. For real, it's our own fault. Like Ralph said, we was too busy ballin' in the club, when we was 'pose to be

lookin' for Tez. Now he's stalking us," Swift stood up, and walked toward the back.
"I'ma show ya'll how to get it done!" J-Nutty shouted after, Swift. He was waving his black Desert Eagle side to side. "Shoulda' come to J-Nutty, you coulda' did it a lot better." He was imitating A-wax off *Menance II Society*.

Swift dug through his bedroom closet, pulling out all kinds of handguns and assault rifles. He tossed each weapon on the bed, then kneeled down to grab a brown box where he kept all the assorted shells. He carried the box over to the bed and sat it down. Swift sat on the edge of the bed and began loading the clips of the various guns. He knew that if anybody was going to stop Tez, it had to be him, out of the crew, Swift had the most bodies under his belt. When he came for you, it was like God sent the angel of death to holla' at you. There was no escaping it. The only problem with Tez though, he wasn't a sitting target. Killing him would be difficult because Swift really didn't know where to find Tez, besides at 007.

Swift slapped the clips into the gun and cocked each one of them, sliding a round into the chamber. He tucked two twin stainless steel 45 semi-autos with the lemon squeeze into the back of his pants, then took it old school with the 9 mm Carrbeam rifle and an all steel, heavy ass Tommy gun, equipped with the fifty round drum packed with 45 dumb bells. Swift grabbed the guns and walked into the front room. He tossed J-Nutty the Tommy gun, while still clutching the Carrbeam. "Damn… I ain't seen this boy in a minute" J-Nutty laughed. He was examining the Tommy, it was partially grey from all the times it had been dropped and the paint peeled. "This mothafucka older than me. You think it still bust?" laughed J-Nutty.
"Nigga, stand in front of it and find out." Swift was pulling his blue hoody over his head.

"This is a fuckin' musket..." laughed J-Nutty. Swift straightened his clothes, pulling his white –T from under his hoody to conceal the two 45's in his back.
"Where we going?" asked J-Nutty.
"To find this bitch-nigga, Tez. And hopefully to bring Tuff home. "I have a feelin' where he's at." Swift grabbed the Carrbeam, and led the way through the house to the side door. They got in J-Nutty's navy blue Charger, and backed out. Swift and J-Nutty, both rode with their rifles on their laps, ducked low in their seats behind the comfort of the tinted windows.

*****

"Get that Yukon right there," Tez pointed to the black GMC Yukon parked near the entrance of Enterprise Rental Car Service located next to Northland Mall.

Lil' One parked the Audi next to the SUV and got out. Tez fired up an L, and turned the radio on low. He nodded to Biggie's 'What's Beef', while getting his plan together. "Beef is when you need to gat's to go to sleep," Tez hummed, as he took a pull off the L. Lil' One came stepping out of the glass door of the rental place, she was carrying the papers to the car and a set of keys. She hit the alarm button on the key chain, and the Yukon sounded with a chirp. Tez snatched Biggie's CD out, and got out of the car.
"Here you go baby," Lil' One handed, Tez the keys to the Yukon.
"A'ight. I want you to follow me to Rosa Parks Middle School, so you can show me the house" Tez said. He took one last pull from the L, then gave Lil' One a shotgun. She swallowed all the smoke as they kissed.
A'ight. Let's get going." Tez pulled away from Lil' One and jumped inside the big boy Yukon.

Tez started the truck, then slid Biggie's CD in, and clicked to 'What's Beef?' "Beef is when I see you.

Guaranteed to be on, I see you…" Tez sang along as he backed out, then skirted out of the parking lot onto Greenfield. He let the sunroof back a little, then leaned his seat back. He looked in the side mirror back at Lil' One, she was right behind him, as they turned onto 8 Mile Road heading back east. Tez still hadn't placed how Tuff knew Pharaoh and how he knew that Pharaoh wanted him dead. These thoughts occupied Tez's mind as he cruised down Gratiot Ave. 'I wonder if all those lil' niggas know who I am, and what's up with me and Pharaoh.' Tez pulled into the parking lot of Rosa Parks Middle School right off Gratiot Ave., on the bend of Outer Drive across the street from old Comerica bank. Kids were playing a game of pick-up basketball. A few heads turned as Lil' One pulled in behind Tez and got out. She was carrying a black duffle bag, held steady at her side. Tez, popped the locks for Lil' One and she climbed in the passenger's seat of the Yukon.
"Where you want me to put this?" asked Lil' One.
"Throw it on the back seat," Tez pulled the neck shift down to drive and did a U-turn. He turned right onto Outer Drive, then took another right down College street.
Lil' One directed, Tez as to where they were going. "Turn right here," she said, as they neared the corner of Rosemary. They both let their seats back and Tez brought the SUV to a steady creep. "That's it right there" Lil' One said, pointing at the house where the crew stayed. Tez looked at the house trying to get a full view, so he could figure out his entry point.
"It don't look like nobody's there" Lil' One said.
"Why you say that?" Tez looked in the rear-view mirror at the house.
"Cause ain't none of their cars there."
"Yeah, you right. Now would be the perfect time." Tez stepped down on the gas and pulled back onto Outer Drive. He turned in the school's parking lot and parked on the side

of the Audi. “How many of them you said it was?” asked Tez.
“Robin, Tuff, J-Nutty and Swift. That’s four” Lil’ One said counting on her fingers. She hadn’t met Ralph.
“A’ight, so that leaves two. I’ma get moving while the house is empty.”
“Be careful,” Lil’ One leaned over and kissed Tez on the lips. She grabbed the door handle, then climbed down from the truck.

Chapter Thirty

Despite the valet parker's death earlier in the day, 007 hadn't missed a beat. Murder was about as common around there as crack on every corner of the city. The police would scrape the body up, ask a few questions and add it to the pile of other unsolved homicides. Swift and J-Nutty sat parked behind Tuff's black Charger. "We been sittin' here for how long, and you still ain't told me what we're waitin' on?" J-Nutty turned to face Swift.

"Who the fuck you think we're waitin' on? We waitin' on that bitch Lil' One or Tez to show up." Swift hadn't taken his eyes off the entrance of the club.

"I gotta use the bathroom. I'ma step inside and see if I see the nigga" J-Nutty said.

"Hurry up" Swift said. J-Nutty got of out the car and crossed the street. Swift watched his back as he entered the club.

"Come on bitch. It's time to die," Swift said looking at the clock on the dashboard. It was going on eleven o'clock.

J-Nutty let the bouncer do a quick little frisk search. The bouncer felt the bulge of the Desert Eagle in J-Nutty's waist.

"I ain't on nothin' big dawg. I'm just using the bathroom and I'm out."

The bouncer looked at J-Nutty side-ways, then nodded toward the bathroom.

"Good-lookin'," J-Nutty scanned the dim-lit club on his way toward the bathroom. He didn't see Tuff anywhere.

"Where the fuck this nigga at?" He pulled the door open to the restroom and stepped in. Some nigga was standing near the sink selling bootleg DVD's and mixtape CD's.

"You tryin' to go, young dawg? I got five for twenty-five. Yo' choice. Mix and match" the ghetto salesman said.

J-Nutty flushed the standing stall, then stepped over to the sink. He looked at all the shit blocking the bowls of the sink and shook his head. He wiped his hands on his pants. "Nah, I'm good."
J-Nutty stepped out of the bathroom and adjusted his eyes to the lights of the club. Chyna pushed him back toward the pay phone on the side of the bathroom. "I knew you'd change yo' mind. What, you missed a pimp the past few days?" J-Nutty asked while back stepping.
Chyna rolled her eyes. "The police is lookin' for ya'll.
"Why would they be lookin' for us?" J-Nutty focused in on Chyna's every word.
"You don't know what happened earlier?" Chyna could tell by the puzzled look on Nutty's face that he didn't.
"Yo' boy, killed the valet driver, then kidnapped that lil' stripper bitch."
"Get the fuck outta here."
"I'm serious. This girl was sittin' in her car, she saw the whole thing and told the police."
"So, why is the hook lookin' for me?"
"Because she told 'em it was one of the 7 Mile Dawgz. They don't know ya'll names, but they passed out their cards to a few people, so I suggest you leave."
J-Nutty looked around the club, then at Chyna. "Yeah. You right. Thank you," he said.

He power walked to the front door, pushing it wide open. He broke into a jog as he hit the parking lot. He crossed the street while looking both ways, reaching the car, he opened the door and flopped down in his seat. He turned the key in the ignition.
"What you doing?" We still waitin'..."
J-Nutty cut, Swift off. "Look, we can't sit out here," he said backing up a little, then pulling out into traffic.
"What's up?" asked Swift.

"Ole' girl I be tryna' holla at, she told me Tuff killed the valet attendant up there earlier, then kidnapped Lil' One."
"What? That explains that yellow crime tape then, huh," Swift said. "But I wonder why he left his car parked out there?"
"He had to leave in Lil' One's car. That's what I'm gettin' from it. Where did he go is the question?" J-Nutty crossed 7 Mile and continued on Outer Drive.
"Oh yeah, ole' girl said the hook is lookin' for us, too. Some bitch saw Tuff snatch Lil' One and told the police it was one of the 7 Mile Dawgz."
"Another mothafucka we gotta kill…"

*****

Tez parked the Yukon on the corner of Rosemary and Outer Drive at Rite Aid Pharmacy. He grabbed the duffle bag off the back seat, and locked the truck up. Tez had taken the alley down to the house on Rosemary. He let himself through the swinging fence, and casually walked up to the back porch of the house. He let himself in through the window inside the covered porch. He had been waiting on Swift and J-Nutty to come home for hours. To keep busy, he searched around the house for anything of value. He found theeir stash of DRO' in the deep freezer, about two hundred pounds. He made plans for the pounds, but left them in the freezer. He found close to $50,000 under Swift's mattress in a brown paper bag. "Nigga's still do this?" said Tez, as he tucked the bag into his pants. He searched the entire house. He was a little hungry, so he decided to raid their fridge. "What ya'll lil' nigga's got to eat." Tez pulled three eggs out of a tray, some sliced cheese, and made himself an omelet.

"Where the fuck these bitch-niggas at?" Tez stood up and flushed the two turds he just dropped. He jiggled the toilet handle, as the bowl clogged up and the turds rose to the top. "Fuck it." Tez closed the lid on the toilet seat, then sparked an L. As he walked through the living room, he heard a car door shut. Then another door shut. "This shit is gettin' crazy" Swift said, as he and J-Nutty climbed the steps of the porch. Tez stomped the blunt out on the floor, and ran toward the back of the house. Swift put his key inside the door, then turned the knob. He pushed the door open and allowed J-Nutty to step in first. "Crazy ain't the word. This nigga is a vet" Swift said. J-Nutty was about to sit the Tommy gun on the coffee table, but he paused in his lean. "You smell that?" He looked around and locked eyes on the smeared blunt ash on the wooden floor. "Somebody's in the house." J-Nutty raised the Tommy, holding it with both hands at waist level he inched toward the dining room. Swift was steps behind him.

Tez was standing in the doorway of the bedroom with his AK-47 pointed toward the end of the hall. *Laaka! Laaka! Laaka!* Tez let off three shots, hitting J-Nutty twice; once in the shoulder, and one in the arm. *Boom! Boom!* J-Nutty let the Tommy come to life as he fell backward from the impact of Tez's 223's. *Laaka! Laaka!* Tez laid on the trigger as he walked down the hall toward the living room. Swift slid into the kitchen. He stood with his back against the wall, while peeking out into the dining room. J-Nutty was on his back with his head propped up, still dumping the Tommy. *Boom! Boom! Boom!* His wild shots tore holes through the dry-wall, but none hit Tez. He, took aim on Nutty's chest and planted a series of shells into his frame. *Laaka!...* Tez was standing over J-Nutty on some overkill shit. He had blanked out.

Baa... Baa... Baa.... Three shots licked off, hitting Tez in his right side. Swift was on Tez's head. He pumped seven more shots into Tez's chest, but Tez remained on his feet. *Click. Click.* Swift dropped the Carrbeam, and went to pull the twin 45's from his back, but Tez took aim and

knocked a patch out of Swift's chest. *Laaka!* Tez walked over to where Swift laid nursing his wound.
"Kill me bitch-nigga!" yelled Swift.
"Oh, you got that comin' but before I kill you, tell me how you know Pharaoh" Tez had his AK pointed down at Swift's head.
"He hired me to kill yo' rat-ass. You can kill me, but you'll be lookin' over your shoulder for the rest of yo' bitch-ass life" Swift yelled.
"Yeah, and you shouda' bought a vest." *Laaka! Laaka!* Tez pumped two slugs into Swift's dome piece. "Nigga, fuck Pharaoh. He'll be to see you in hell soon," Tez assured Swift, then kicked him hard in the rib cage. "Fuck, Pharaoh!"

Chapter Thirty-one

Ralph promised Pharaoh before leaving that he would keep things in the street, and not bring Tez's Ma' Dukes into the beef.

"Call me when you get back and let me know what's good," Pharaoh gave Ralph dap.

"A'ight" Ralph said.

He climbed behind the wheel of the 430 Lex and cruised the shoreline to the bridge. Ralph pushed send, after scrolling down his phone log on his cell to Swift's number. He flashed his license at the customs agent and was waved across the bridge. Swift's phone vibrated on his hip as he lay dead on the dining room floor. Ralph closed his cell shut, as he turned down Jefferson Ave. It was almost two o'clock in the morning, so Ralph figured them niggas were probably passed out in the living room from smoking and drinking. He relaxed and turned up the radio. As he turned the corner of Rosemary, Ralph could see J-Nutty's Charger in the driveway, but he didn't see Tuff's Charger. 'Fuck this nigga at?' Ralph thought, as he pulled across the street and parked. He cut the engine, then got out of the car. His neighbor, Ms. Rose saw him pull up and stepped out on the front porch.

"Hi, Ms. Rose" Ralph said smiling, as he started for the steps.

"Ralph, I wouldn't go in there if I were you," warned Ms. Rose. She was a little old lady. She stood no more than four feet, and was at least 70 years old. She brushed her silver hair to the side of her face, then wrapped it around her ear.

"What's wrong, Ms. Rose?" Ralph cut across the lawn and stopped on the side of Ms. Rose's house.

"I heard gunshots coming out that house. They started a few minutes after Jamar and Manny got back. Ms. Rose called all them by their real names.
"How long ago was this?" asked Ralph, turning to look at the house.
"About two hours ago. I called the police, but they never showed up."
"Thank you, Ms. Rose." Ralph started for the house.
"Hold on. I can't let you go by yourself. Let me get my stick." Ms. Rose scooted inside the house, then back out the door toting a stick about as big as her. "This my nigga-beater," she said falling in step with Ralph.

Ralph slid his 40 cal. from the waist of his pants as they reached the landing. He twisted the door knob and slowly pushed the door open. Ms. Rose held her stick above her head, as she inched behind Ralph through the living room. Ralph dropped his gun to his side at the sight of Swift's eyes looking up at him from the dining room. "Oh my Jesus…" said Ms. Rose, stopping next to Ralph. She wrapped her arm around Ralph's waist, and tried to console him. Ralph dropped to his knees and buried his face in the floor. He sobbed in disbelief, not Swift. They were like brothers. "Oh, Ralph." Ms. Rose kneeled beside him and rubbed his back while he cried his eyes out. "He killed, Swift…" cried Ralph. "It's going to be okay, baby. Jesus."
Ralph wasn't trying to hear anything about Jesus, Luke, David, Mark or none of those other niggas. Murder was the only thing on his mind. He raised up from the puddle of tears and took one long look at Swift and J-Nutty, then walked out of the house."Ralph, don't you go and do nothin' that's gone get you in trouble." Ms. Rose was following behind Ralph, she stopped at the curb as Ralph climbed inside the Lexus and peeled away from the curb.

Ralph looked in the rear-view mirror. “All deals are off,” he said with a cold stare.

Chapter Thirty-two

Ralph pulled an all-nighter. He parked across the street from Al's Barber shop in front of BB's Diner and waited through the wee-hours until the shop opened. Maurice, Al's youngest son, pulled into the parking lot of the shop and parked his 420 Benz. He got out of the car and reached in the back seat for his briefcase containing his clippers and blades. Ralph got out of the Lexus and crossed 7 Mile Road. He approached Mo' who was walking with his head down. Ralph startled Mo', he skidded back on his Hush Puppies, making a scratching sound against the concrete.

"Back up, young blood," Maurice had pulled his baby 380 out of his side holster and took aim at Ralph's torso.

"Mo', it's me, Ralph. Trina's son."

"What you want?" asked Maurice, he slowly lowered his pistol, then put it back in his holster.

"I want to talk to you about someone."

Maurice started toward the shop. "I cut hair for a living, not sell information."

Ralph stopped behind Maurice as he fiddled with the full key ring. "Mo', I believe you have good enough reason to be interested" he said, following Mo' inside the shop.

"Lock that door, and turn that light switch on," ordered Mo', as he walked over to his workstation. He slid the door open to his sanitizer and flipped the latches on his briefcase. "Go head, I'm listening."

"I don't know if you know this or not, but I'm Pharaoh's lil' guy. I'm helping him with some thangs," Ralph took a seat in Mo's barber chair.

"You getting a cut?" asked Mo'.

"You did say that you cut hair for a living, and not sell info. So, we can kill two birds with one stone."
Mo', flipped his cape around Ralph's neck, then put a white neck tie around him and fastened the cape. "How you want it?"
"Full taper."
Mo', began running his comb through Ralph's scalp. "So, how's old Pharaoh?" Mo', turned his adjustable clippers on and started fading Ralph's hair.
"He'd be a lot better if Tez weren't tryin' to send him to prison for life."
"I hate that rat-fucker. Somebody needs to find him and kill his ass," Mo' said with emotion.
"That's where I come in. Listen, Mo' I heard about when Tez made everybody strip naked and robbed the crap game. I know you still want some justice."
"Do I?"
"Well, I'ma give it to you. I need your help though, finding the bastard. Where does his mother live?"
"Oh, Brenda. She stays over on Justine. Matter of fact, she lives two houses down from a rental property I got over there."
"Between what side streets?" asked Ralph.
"Emery and Lance. She got a bunch of flower pots on the landing of her porch. You can't miss it. It's 'bout the fourth house from the corner on your right hand side." Mo', stopped cutting Ralph's hair to demonstrate with his hands. "I hope you get that slimy sona-bitch."
"Oh, I've got a feeling I will."

Ralph had all the information he needed. He paid Mo' for the cut and thanked him for the information. He exited Al's and crossed the street and jumped inside the Lexus. He pulled into the morning traffic and drove west on 7 Mile. Ralph wasn't wasting any time on getting even. He made a right down Justine and crossed Emery, he let the

Lexus coast as he zeroed in on Tez's momma's house. It was just the way Maurice had described it. Plants hung from the roof of the porch and large white flower pots decorated the stone railings. Ralph bent the block and came back around. He parked on the corner of Emery, and got out of the car. He put his hands inside his pockets where his 40 cal. rested. He caressed the butt of his gun, while walking at a steady pace up Justine. Ralph walked up the long cement strip, leading to the steps of the porch. He took the steps two at a time, reaching the landing Ralph took a look down the block, then reached for the doorbell. *Ding-Dong! Ding-Dong!*
"I'm coming!" she paused the DVD, then sat the remote back on the coffee table. "Who is this early as it is?" Brenda patted the beads of sweat from her forehead, as she walked toward the front door. "Who is it?"
Ralph grabbed the handle to the screen door, and pulled it open. "A friend of Tez's."
Brenda, heard Tez's name and yanked the door open. "Who are you?"
Ralph came out his pocket with the 40 cal. and pointed it to Brenda's stomach. "I said, a friend of Tez." Ralph forced Brenda back inside the house.
"Please don't hurt me. I know…"
"Bitch, shut the fuck up," ordered Ralph.

Ralph closed the front door behind him, as he turned his head, Brenda charged him. She tried some of that yoga/karate shit out on Ralph, as she climbed on his back. She was fighting for her life, trying to dig Ralph's eyes out. "Ahh!..." yelled Ralph. He twisted and turned, trying to free himself from Brenda's death grip. She was locked on his back like a backpack. Ralph rammed her into the wall hard, then flipped her off his back. Brenda crashed to the floor scraping her head against the carpet. Ralph, reached down and slapped Brenda across the face with the barrel of his gun. "You old bitch. I'll kill you!" Ralph grabbed Brenda by her hair and twisted it around his fist. He stood her up while still clutching her hair. Ralph walked her over to the telephone sitting on a stand beside the sofa. "Here," he said, handing Brenda the receiver. "Get Tez on the phone, now!" ordered Ralph.

"Please don't kill me," pleaded Brenda, as she dialed Tez's cell number.

"Shut the fuck up and do like I tell you."

"Hold on. It's for you," Lil' One passed Tez his cell.

"Who this?" asked Tez.

"It's your mother. Martez, some man is here at the house. He has me at gunpoint, and wants to speak with you. Tez, what's going on?"

Tez hadn't budged from his comfortable little nook next to Lil' One. They were laid up in bed blowing some of the DRO' he took from Robin. "I mean, what do you want me to do, Ma?"

"You need to get over here!"

"For what? Ain't no sense in both of us dying. Matter fact, put the nigga on the phone."

"Hello!" yelled Ralph.

"Nigga, who is this?" asked Tez.

"That's beside the point. Bitch-nigga, I got yo' mom's and if you ever want to see her alive again, you'd meet me…"

"Dawg, check this out," Tez cut Ralph short. "Like I told her, ain't no sense in both us dying. So, I'm not meeting you nowhere. Do what you do, and catch me in traffic," Tez said, then hung up. Ralph looked at the phone, then hung it up.

"Did ya'll settle whatever it is ya'll feuding about?" asked Brenda.

Ralph put the 40 cal. to the side of Brenda's temple. "Yeah" he said, then blew Brenda's brains out. *Boom!*

"Baby, who was that on the phone?" Lil' One curled back under Tez's arm.
"My mom."
"Oh, how she doin'?"
"Some nigga got her at gunpoint he tryna' do some trade-off shit. Her for me." Tez fired up another blunt and took smoke through his nose. He leaned back on the pillow and looked up to the ceiling.
Lil' One sat up quickly. "What? Let's go get her!"
"Calm down, baby" Tez said, taking another pull from the L.
"Calm down! What are you going to do, just lay here?"
"My momma done lived her life. If he kills her, I'ma make it even." Tez showed no emotion whatsoever. 'It's all fair game,' Tez thought.

Chapter Thirty-Three

Death never bothered Ralph before, because of all the people he had watched die, he didn't care about them. He could squeeze the trigger in a heartbeat and take someone's life, and have not a second thought about it, just like any other killer. But, the difference between Ralph and Tez, was that Tez didn't care about anyone, not even his own mom, so how could you beat a nigga like him? Tez played the game raw, when it was yo' time to go, that's what it was, but he wasn't about to die early on the strength of anybody.

With blood on his hands, Ralph was still thirsty. Killing Brenda hadn't brought him any type of closure. Ralph gripped the wheel of the Lexus with both hands while flying down 7 Mile Road. He was on his way to the warehouse on Neveda. Ralph knew once Pharaoh found out about Brenda, he'd probably stop fucking with him and maybe even want to kill him. Ralph pulled into the alley behind the warehouse. He parked the car, then jumped out, rushing to the back slider gate. He wresteled with the lock for a moment and the handle on the garage door, then pulled it up. Ralph rushed back to his car and put his lights on. He pulled inside the warehouse to the middle of the floor and shut the engine off. He got out of the car and walked toward the garage door. He reached up for the long battered string, then pulled the door shut. He went straight to work loading what was left of the hydro into the trunk of the Lexus, and put some bales on the back seat. There were about 250 pounds left. He packed all the weed in the car, then took a final look around the warehouse. Ralph pulled the garage door up, then backed out the Lexus. He peeled out down the alley, leaving the warehouse wide open. He made a right at the end of the alley onto Keystone Street. Ralph looked in the rear-view mirror to see if anyone had seen him. He focused back on the road, as he crossed 7 Mile, keeping straight on Keystone. He stopped by his apartment on 10 Mile and Conant to grab his stash of money and some clothes. He stuffed his clothes in the back seat, then hid the money underneath the hood of the car. He climbed behind the wheel and did a U-turn heading back toward 8 Mile. He flipped open his cell phone and scrolled through the names. He stopped on Maxine, then pushed send.

"Hello?"

"What's up, baby? It's Ralph."

"Oh, hey. How you doing? When am I going to see you again?" asked Max.

"Hopefully, in a couple of hours. I'm turning onto the highway now."

"Well, I'll be here waiting on you," Max said excited.

"In a minute. Bye."

Ralph closed his cell phone and strapped his seat belt on as he rode down the ramp to I-94. He was on his way to Saginaw, Michigan. He had met Maxine on one of his trips with Swift when they were trying to make new contacts. Maxine was a thick bow-legged, brown skinned chick with a fat ass and some nice sized titties, She had this sexy-ass gap between her teeth, not to mention the one between her legs. Ralph got the pussy once, the night he met her. He had promised Max they would hook back up, seeing as though all his niggas were dead, and Pharaoh would be looking for him, what better time than now. Ralph was straight. He had his money and 250 poundds of DRO'. He didn't have to ever look back.

Chapter Thirty-Four

Lil' One was still in her feelings. She couldn't believe that Tez would sit back and let somebody kill his mother. Lil' One was starting to look at Tez in another light, because if he'd let his own mother get killed, Lil' One knew what he'd do for her. She was so mad that she refused to share the bed with Tez, so he made her go sleep on the sofa in the front room. Tez slept like a baby. He hadn't missed a wink of sleep, even after verifying that Brenda was killed. Tez stretched and yawned, as he rolled onto his back. His eyes adjusted to the sun rays beaming through the bedroom window. He stared up at the ceiling briefly, then reached for the blunt and lighter on the night stand. He flicked the lighter and held the flame at the tip of the L, while rotating the blunt in a circular motion. Tez took a long pull off the L, then snatched the sheets off his legs. He sat on the edge of the bed for a second, then slid into his house shoes. He dressed while killing the last of the blunt. He stepped into the bathroom and washed his face and then back into the bedroom to grab his trusted 40 cal. Walking into the living room, Tez tucked his gun in his waist and pulled his hoody over the handle, he shook Lil' One's leg as she lay asleep on the sofa.

"What, Tez?" asked Lil' One, she still had an attitude.

"Oh, you still trippin' 'bout yesterday? You didn't even know my mom" Tez yelled, as he stared down at Lil' One.

"But that's yo' mother. Do you love me, Tez?" Lil' One sat up to face Tez. She looked deep into his eyes as he spoke.

"Of course I love you. But will I die for you? Hell nah. That shit goes for my mom, my kids, yo' ass and anybody else. 'Cause ain't nobody gone die for me. I wouldn't even expect them to. But like I told you last night. I'ma make it even." Tez turned to leave.

"Where are you going?"

The door slammed as Tez stepped into the hallway of the complex. He exited the building and walked to his Audi. He popped the locks and climbed behind the wheel. Tez sparked another blunt as he cruised down Petersburg Blvd. He was on his way to Royal Oak, Michigan. He flipped through his CD case and pulled Biggie's 2nd LP out, 'Life after Death' disc two. Tez put the CD in and skipped to 'What's Beef?' He had to set the mood for what would follow.

Tez pulled into Bald Hills private community of Royal Oak, Michigan. The Audi was engulfed by huge oak trees which lined both sides of the street. As Tez drove down Naples Street he locked eyes on a recently built snow white colonial-style mansion just two properties to his right. Tez pulled into the driveway and parked behind the lavender 500 SL Mercedes that sat parked in front of the garage. Tez took a long pull from the L, then sat it in the ashtray. "Beef is when yo' mom's ain't safe up in the street…" Tez sang along to the chorus. He cut the car off, then pushed the door open. Tez was no stranger to the mansion. He ate dinner there on several occasions, and even spent a few holidays there. He walked around the side of the estate and grabbed the screen door handle to the greenhouse. Tez stepped inside the greenhouse and walked over to the adjacent door leading to the main house. He turned the knob and let himself in. He walked through the formal dining room, and into the arcade room.

"What's up lil' man?" asked Tez.

"Uncle, Tez!" The little boy ran over to Tez and jumped into his arms.

"Where's your grandma?" Tez asked, holding the boy in his arms.

"Upstairs. You bring me anything?" asked the little boy.
"Of course, I did," Tez sat him down, then dug in his pocket and gave the boy two hundreds.
"Thank you, uncle Tez."
"You're welcome. Let me go see 'bout grandma." The little boy rushed back over to the *Grand Theft Auto* arcade game he'd been playing. Tez started up the marble staircase.

*****

"So, you're going to run for the rest of your life? It's not fair to Jr. you know. He's asking me about you more and more everyday…"
"Ma, I'm not going to run forever. I just have some things that must be taken care of before I face the music."
"You know your momma is not stupid. I know what's going on, and it's truly a shame. But I understand. You do what you must, so we can be a family again."

Tez pulled his 40 cal. from his waist and crept down the hall toward the master bedroom. He could hear his target's voice talking on the phone…
"Oh, my God!"
"Momma, what's wrong?" asked Pharaoh.
Boom! Boom! Boom! Boom!
"Momma!" yelled Pharaoh after the gun shots ceased. He held the phone to his ear waiting for a response from Ma' Dukes. "Momma!..."
Tez walked over and picked the phone up from the bed.
"Momma!" yelled Pharaoh.
"What up doe" Tez said coldly. Pharaoh's heart sunk. He knew that voice anywhere. "Now we're even" Tez said, then slammed the phone on the hook…

Stay tuned for Part III

Sample Chapters

From Hoodfellas

By
Richard Jeanty

Chapter 1

The Natural Course

"Mr. Brown, we're not really here to negotiate with you. It's more like a demand, or whatever you wanna call it," said Crazy D.

"What makes you think I'm gonna do what you're telling me to do?" Mr. Brown asked. "Yo, Short Dawg, bring her out," Crazy D ordered.

Short Dawg appeared from behind Mr. Brown's storage area with a knife to Mr. Brown's wife's neck while her left hand is covered in blood. "She still has nine good fingers left, but next time we won't be cutting off fingers, oh no, we ain't interested in the same body part twice. Next time it might be one of her eyeballs hanging out the socket," Crazy D said as he signaled for Short Dawg to bring the knife to Mrs. Brown's eyes. "Tell me what you want and I'll do it, just don't hurt her," said Mr. Brown. "We've been watching you for a while now and my guesstimation is that you make about fifty to a hundred thousand dollars a month. Forty percent of that is ours and we're gonna collect it on every first of the month," he said. "How we supposed to survive? The shop doesn't even make that kind of money," Mr. Brown pleaded. "Do you need motivation to make that kind of money?" Crazy D asked as he raised his hand to Short Dawg, ordering him to start taking out one of Mrs. Brown's eyes. Before he could stick the knife in, Mr. Brown chimed in and said, "Okay, I'll do it. I'll give you forty percent of what we make." Crazy D smiled and said, "No, you'll give me forty percent of a hundred thousand dollars every month. He ordered Short Dawg to drop the knife with a swift movement of his head.

As Crazy D and Short Dawg were making their way out of the shop, Mr. Brown reached for his shotgun. However, before he could cock it back, Crazy D had his .45 Lugar in his face saying, "It's your choice, old man, you can die a hero or you can become a zero." Mr. Brown wisely placed his shotgun down, and then apologized to Crazy D. What Crazy D did to thc Browns was routine since he came out of the State Pen. Crazy D walked out of jail wearing some donated clothes that were twenty years out of style and fit a little too snug around his six foot-plus frame. The difference this time was the tightness of the fit. He had gained a considerable amount of weight in muscle. The shirt was tight around his arms and his pants barely made it past his thighs. He was ridiculed as he rode the bus back to his old neighborhood. The kids were pointing at him, adults shook their heads at him and women just laughed at him. Crazy D was fed up with the treatment he received his first day out of jail. He looked like a buff homo. With no money and no skills to get a job, Crazy D had no choice but to turn back to a life of crime. After serving a twenty-year sentence for robbery and second-degree murder, the system failed him miserably, but even worse, they failed the rest of society by letting a loose canon out of jail without the proper rehabilitation.

While in jail, Crazy D's mom only visited him the first few months. She soon fell victim to the crack epidemic and ultimately had to turn her back on her son at his request. There came a time when she could hardly remember that she had a son. While constantly under the influence of crack cocaine, his mother did her own stint in prison for prostitution and other petty crimes only to get out and start using again.

Crazy D went to jail at the young age of seventeen and it was there that he learned his survival tactics. Wreaking havoc on people before they got to him was what he learned when he was in prison. The attempted rape on him the first week after he arrived at the Walpole facility in Massachusetts brought his awareness to a level he never knew existed. He was lucky that one of the toughest inmates in that prison was a friend of his father's. Word had gotten out that Crazy D was being shipped to Walpole and his father's best friend made a promise to his mother to look after him. Crazy D's dad, Deon Sr., and Mean T were best friends before his dad got killed, and Mean T was sent to prison for thirty years after a botched armed robbery against a store owner.

Chapter 2

Mean T and Sticky Fingers

Mean T and Sticky Fingers aka Deon Campbell Sr. were best friends throughout their entire lives. They were more like vagrants from the time their mother decided to allow them to walk to school by themselves. In fact, the very first day that they walked to school without any supervision, they decided to make a detour to the corner store. Mean T was the lookout while Sticky Fingers robbed the store of candy, potato chips, juices and other valuables that matter to kids. It was a little distance from Evans Street to Morton Street in Dorchester, Massachusetts, but their parents trusted that they would walk directly to school everyday. The Taylor Elementary School was where most of the kids who lived on the Dorchester side of Morton Street went to school. Stealing became a fun habit for the duo and every morning they found themselves down the block at the corner store stealing more items than their pockets could afford. Mean T was the bigger of the two, but Sticky Fingers was the conniving thief. He could steal the bible from a preacher, and Mean T would knock the daylights out of a pregnant woman.

Over the years, the duo broaden their horizons from stealing candy to stealing sneakers and clothes out of a store called 42nd Street located in Mattapan Square. By then, they were in high school being promoted because of their age and not the work that they did. The two were dumb as a doorknob, but one was an expert thief and the other an enforcer. The two friends were the best young hustlers from their block. The Korean owner of the store was forced to install cameras because Sticky Fingers and Mean T kept robbing the store and there was never any proof to prosecute them. Usually, the cops didn't respond on time and by then the two had made it home safely with their stolen goods. The shop owner was growing tired of this and decided to arm himself in order to keep from getting robbed.

Mean T and Sticky Fingers wore the freshest gear to school. Everything was brand name because they stole the best of everything from the different stores downtown Boston. Their favorite stores were Filene's, Jordan Marsh, Filene's Basement and of course, 42nd Street in Mattapan Square. On top of that, the two of them sold some of the stolen merchandise to some of the kids at the high school when they needed money. Their bad habit became an enterprise. The two thieves outfitted their bedrooms with stolen goods from stores all over the Boston area. They had enough merchandise to supply a whole high school of kids with clothes, shoes and other clothing items such as socks, t-shirts, underwear and long johns needed for at least a month. However, Mean T and Sticky Fingers would run into some difficulty when they decided to rob the 42nd Street store once more. The Korean owner had had enough and he felt he needed to protect his livelihood, so he bought a gun.

By this time, Mean T and Sticky Fingers were pretty known to the entire Korean family who worked as a unit in the store. While Sticky Fingers walked around and stuffed his bag with stolen items, so he could dash out of the store using the same tactics they had used in the past with Mean T knocking out the father who stood guard at the entrance, the father looked on. However, on this day, they would meet their fate. As Sticky Fingers rushed towards the exit, all he felt was a hot bullet piercing through his heart. Mean T didn't even have time to react as the small Korean man raised his gun and stuck it in Mean T's mouth. Pandemonium rang out in the store as everyone tried to make it to the exit. Meanwhile, Sticky Finger's lifeless body lay on the ground with his hands clutched around a duffle bag filled with stolen items. The cops arrived in no time. Someone's life had to be taken in order for the cops to respond in a timely manner.

Mr. Chang, as the community later found out the store owner's name, had to defend himself against the whole community. No one came to his defense when he was being robbed blindly, but everyone was angry because another young black life had been taken. Sticky Finger's mom came out shedding tears as if she didn't know what her son was doing in the street. A search of the victim's home revealed about fifty thousand dollars worth of stolen items from different stores, including Mr. Chang's 42nd Street. Sticky Finger's mom had to have known that her son was hawking stolen merchandise because the officers could barely take a step into his room without stepping over stolen clothes while serving the search warrant. The whole place was cluttered with clothes scattered all over the room.

To top off an already insane situation, the cops found a loaded gun on Mean T after searching him at the scene. Mean T aka Tony Gonsalves, an American born Cape Verde heritage young man was handcuffed and taken to jail where he faced aggravated robbery, illegal possession of a handgun, first degree armed robbery and a list of other charges concocted by the district attorney to ensure his proper place away from society for the next thirty years. It didn't help that Tony and Deon weren't in good standing at school. No teachers, counselor or principal would vouch for them as good people. The media smeared their names even further and there was no way that Tony was going to walk even though his friend was killed.

A few months after Deon's murder, the media revealed that he had left behind a pregnant woman with an unborn child. That child would be named Deon after his father. Mean T would receive a thirty-year sentence, the maximum allowed under

Massachusetts law. He was transferred from the correctional facility in Concord to the facility in Walpole after his sentence. As a young man, Mean T didn't really understand the extent of his sentence, so he chose to act in a machismo way and accepted his fate. On the van ride from Concord to Walpole, while shackled to other hardcore criminals, reality started to set in for Mean T and he understood clearly that his life had taken a drastic turn for the worst and he had better start thinking about his survival tactics. Mean T rose to prominence very quickly at the prison as he engaged some of the tougher inmates in fights and defeated quite a few of them while earning their respect.

Mean T was tested the very day he was headed to Walpole to start his sentence. One repeated offender wanted to impress all the impressionable first timers in the van, and he made the unthinkable mistake of picking on Meant T.

"You're gonna be my bitch when we touch down," he said to Mean T with a tempted grin. The whole van was laughing except Meant T. He was sitting in the row in front of Mean T and had to turn his neck around to talk to him. Before he could turn around to say something else, Mean T threw his handcuffed hands around his neck and choked him until he passed out. Words had gotten around about the incident and Mean T was given his props for almost killing a man who was known as Nutty Harold in prison. Nutty Harold was released on a technicality and he unfortunately had a confrontation with Mean T on his way back to prison after killing a man six months out of prison.

It was almost eighteen years later, a few months short of his eighteenth birthday, when Crazy D aka Deon Campbell Jr. would walk into the prison in Walpole to meet the guardian angel known to him as Abdul Mustafa Muhammad. Mean T had converted to Islam while serving his sentence. He had gotten into many fights after arriving at the prison, including one that involved sending a prison guard to the emergency room, which earned him an additional ten years to his sentence. Mean T was casually walking to his cell after code red was called. This one particular guard, who hated him for garnering the respect of his fellow inmates, felt Mean T was not walking fast enough. He used his stick to rush Mean T back to his cell thinking that the other two guards behind him provided a safe haven from an asswhip. Mean T was much too quick and strong for the guard as he found his neck wrapped inside Mean T's massive biceps. The two guards stood back as Mean T threatened to choke the life out of the guard who unjustly pushed and hit him with the stick. The white guard started turning pink and his eyes bulging out of their sockets as he fainted from the chokehold feeling that life itself was about to end. The other two guards could only watch in horror before stepping in to provide some relief for the guard using their night stick. He became a lifer. Abdul, formerly known as Tony Gonsalves also formerly known as Mean T on the streets, was a highly respected man in prison. As a lifer, he had earned the reputation of a tough, intelligent and manipulating leader. He protected those close to him and destroyed those who went against him.

Serosa becomes the subject to information that could financially ruin and possibly destroy the lives and careers of many prominent people involved in the government if this data is exposed. As this intricate plot thickens, speculations start mounting and a whirlwind of death, deceit, and betrayal finds its way into the ranks of a once impenetrable core of the government. Will Serosa fall victim to the genetic structure that indirectly binds her to her parents causing her to realize there s NO WAY OUT!

In Stores!!!

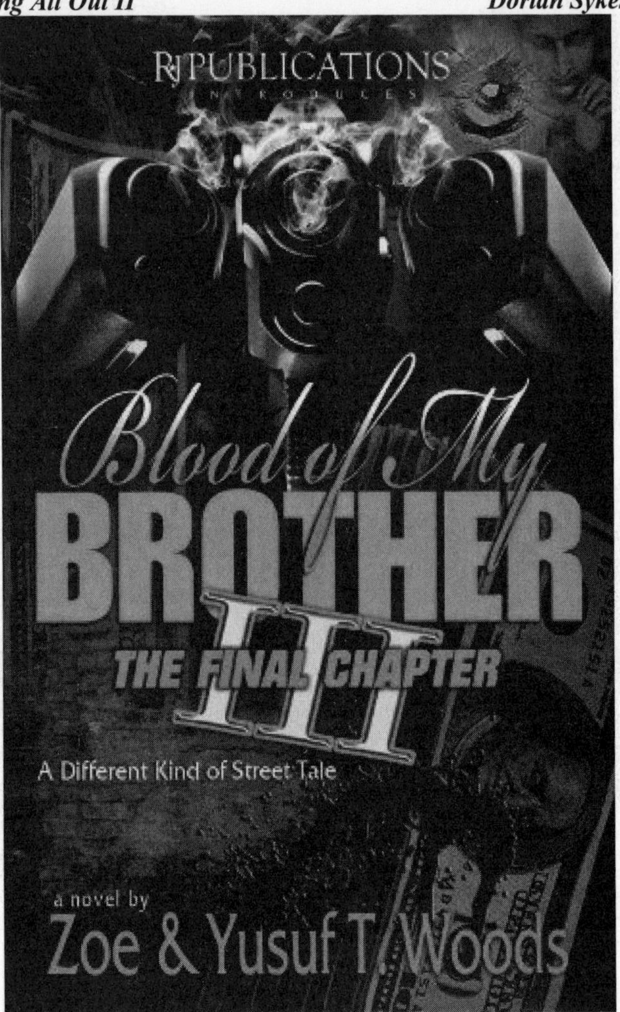

Retiring is no longer an option for Roc, who is now forced to restudy Philly's vicious streets through blood filled eyes. He realizes that his brother's killer is none other than his mentor, Mr. Holmes. With this knowledge, the strategic game of chess that began with the pushing of a pawn in the Blood of My Brother series, symbolizes one of love, loyalty, blood, mayhem, and death. In the end, the streets of Philadelphia will never be the same...

In Storess!!!

After Chasin' Satisfaction, Julius finds that satisfaction is not all that it's cracked up to be. It left nothing but death in its aftermath. Now living the glamorous life in Miami while putting the finishing touches on his hybrid condo hotel, he realizes with newfound success he's now become the hunted. Julian's success is threatened as someone from his past vows revenge on him.

In Stores!!!

It may not be Histeria Lane, but these desperate housewives are fed up with their neglecting husbands. Their sexual needs take precedence over the millions of dollars their husbands bring home every year to keep them happy in their affluent neighborhood. While their husbands claim to be hard at work, these wives are doing a little work of their own with the bedroom bandit. Is the bandit swift enough to evade these angry husbands?

In Stores!!

NEGLECTED SOULS

Motherhood and the trials of loving too hard and not enough frame this story...The realism of these characters will bring tears to your spirit as you discover the hero in the villain you never saw coming...

In Stores!!!

Jimmy and Nina continue to feel a void in their lives because they haven't a clue about their genealogical make-up. Jimmy falls victims to a life threatening illness and only the right organ donor can save his life. Will the donor be the bridge to reconnect Jimmy and Nina to their biological family? Will Nina be the strength for her brother in his time of need? Will they ever find out what really happened to their mother?

In Stores!!!

Betrayal, lust, lies, murder, deception, sex and tainted love frame this story... Julian Stevens lacks the ambition and freak ability that Miko looks for in a man, but she married him despite his flaws to spite an ex-boyfriend. When Miko least expects it, the old boyfriend shows up and ready to sweep her off her feet again. She wants to have her cake and eat it too. While Miko's doing her own thing, Julian is determined to become everything Miko ever wanted in a man and more, but will he go to extreme lengths to prove he's worthy of Miko's love? Julian Stevens soon finds out that he's capable of being more than he could ever imagine as he embarks on a journey that will change his life forever.

In Stores!!!

The police in New York and other major cities around the country are increasingly victimizing black men. The violence has escalated to deadly force, most of the time without justification. In this controversial book, noted author Richard Jeanty, tackles the problem of police brutality and the unfair treatment of Black men at the hands of police in New York City and the rest of the country.

In Stores!!!

Just when Darren thinks his relationship with Tina is flourishing, there is yet another hurdle on the road hindering their bliss. Tina saw a therapist for months to deal with her sexual addiction, but now Darren is wondering if she was ever treated completely. Darren has not been taking care of home and Tina's frustrated and agrees to a break-up with Darren. Will Darren lose Tina for good? Will Tina ever realize that Darren is the best man for her?

In Stores!!

Ronald Murphy was a player all his life until he and his best friend, Myles, met the women of their dreams during a brief vacation in South Beach, Florida. Sexual Jeopardy is story of trust, betrayal, forgiveness, friendship and hope.

In Stores!!!

Tina develops an insatiable sexual appetite very early in life. She only loves her boyfriend, Darren, but he's too far away in college to satisfy her sexual needs.
Tina decides to get buck wild away in college
Will her sexual trysts jeopardize the lives of the men in her life?

In Stores!!!

Faith Jones, a woman in her mid-thirties, has given up on ever finding love again until she met her son's best friend, Darius. Faith Jones is walking a thin line of betrayal against her son for the love of Darius. Will Faith allow her emotions to outweigh her common sense?

In Stores!!!

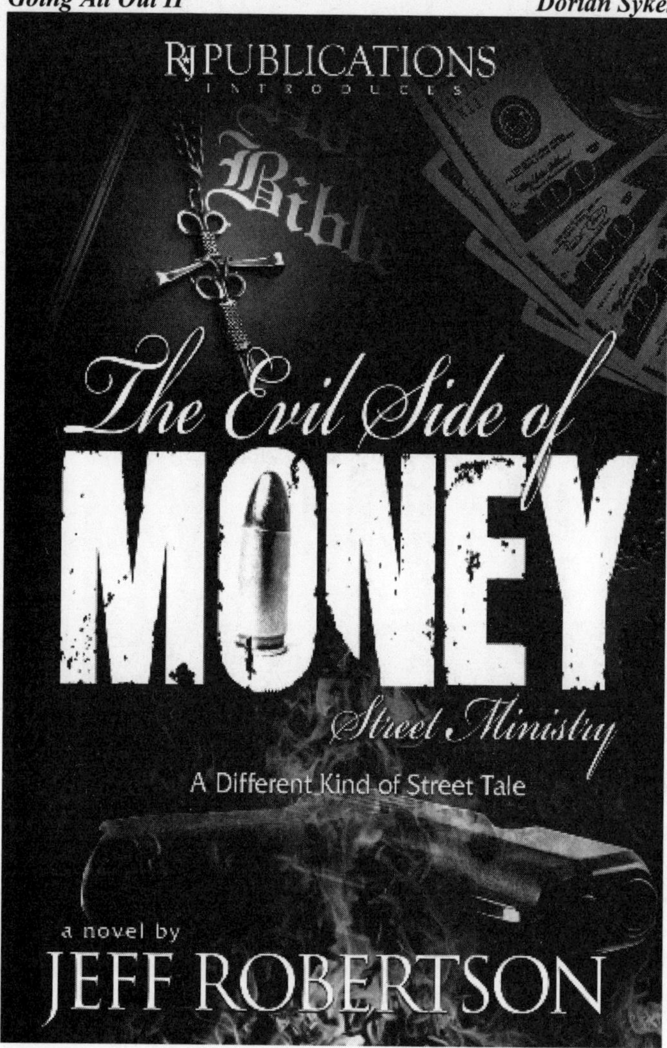

Violence, Intimidation and carnage are the order as Nathan and his brother set out to build the most powerful drug empires in Chicago. However, when God comes knocking, Nathan's conscience starts to surface. Will his haunted criminal past get the best of him?

In Stores!!

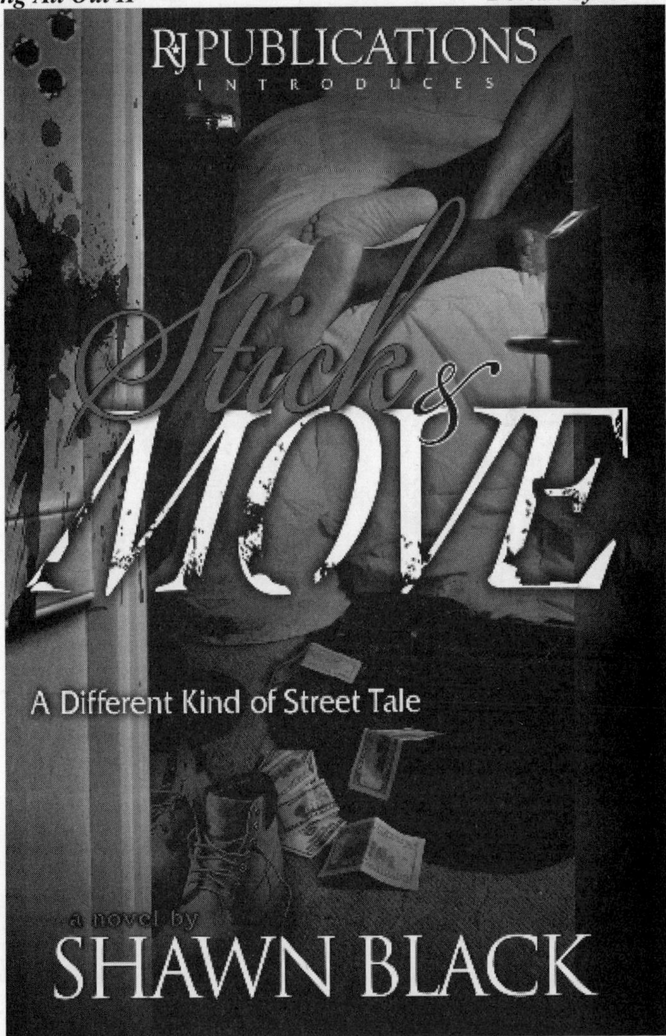

Yasmina witnessed the brutal murder of her parents at a young age at the hand of a drug dealer. This event stained her mind and upbringing as a result. Will Yamina's life come full circle with her past? Find out as Yasmina's crew, The Platinum Chicks, set out to make a name for themselves on the street.

In stores!!

Ashland's mother, Bianca, fights hard to suppress the truth from her daughter because she doesn't want her to marry Jordan, the grandson of an ex-lover she loathes. Ashland soon finds out how cruel and vengeful her mother can be, but what price will Bianca pay for redemption?

In stores!!

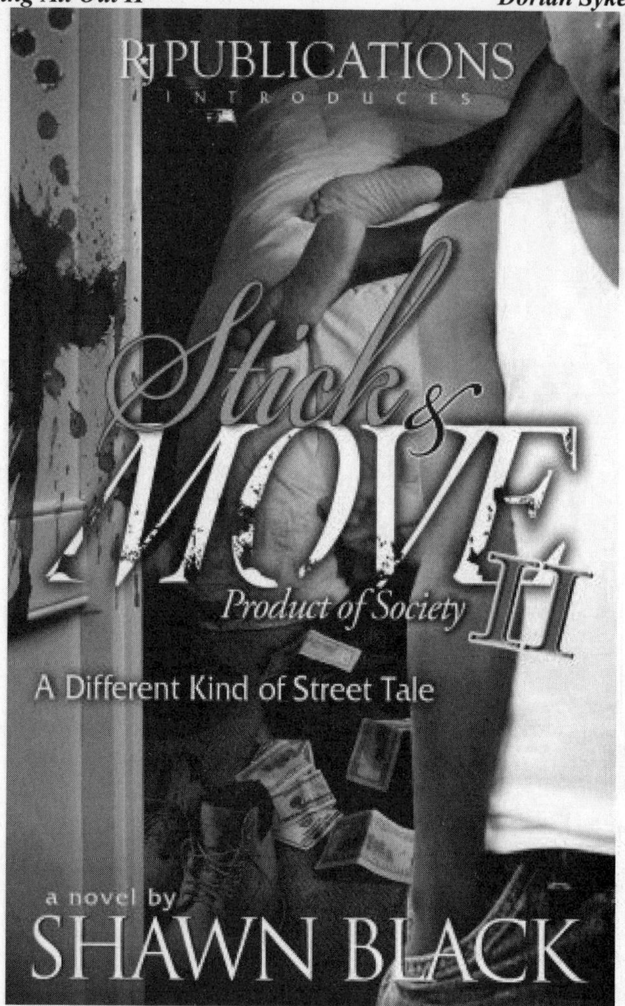

Scorcher and Yasmina's low key lifestyle was interrupted when they were taken down by the Feds, but their daughter, Serosa, was left to be raised by the foster care system. Will Serosa become a product of her environment or will she rise above it all? Her bloodline is undeniable, but will she be able to control it?

In Stores!!

An ex-drug dealer finds himself in a bind after he's caught by the Feds. He has to decide which is more important, his family or his loyalty to the game. As he fights hard to make a decision, those who helped him to the top fear the worse from him. Will he get the chance to tell the govt. whole story, or will someone get to him before he becomes a snitch?

In Stores!!!

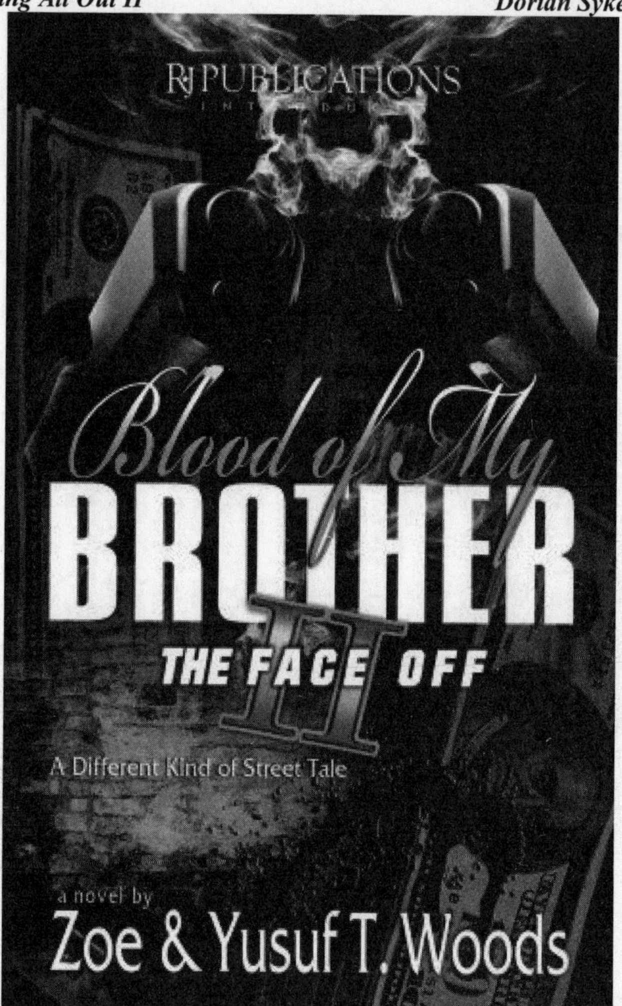

What will Roc do when he finds out the true identity of Solo? Will the blood shed come from his own brother Lil Mac? Will Roc and Solo take their beef to an explosive height on the street? Find out as Zoe and Yusuf bring the second installment to their hot street joint, Blood of My Brother.

In Stores!!!

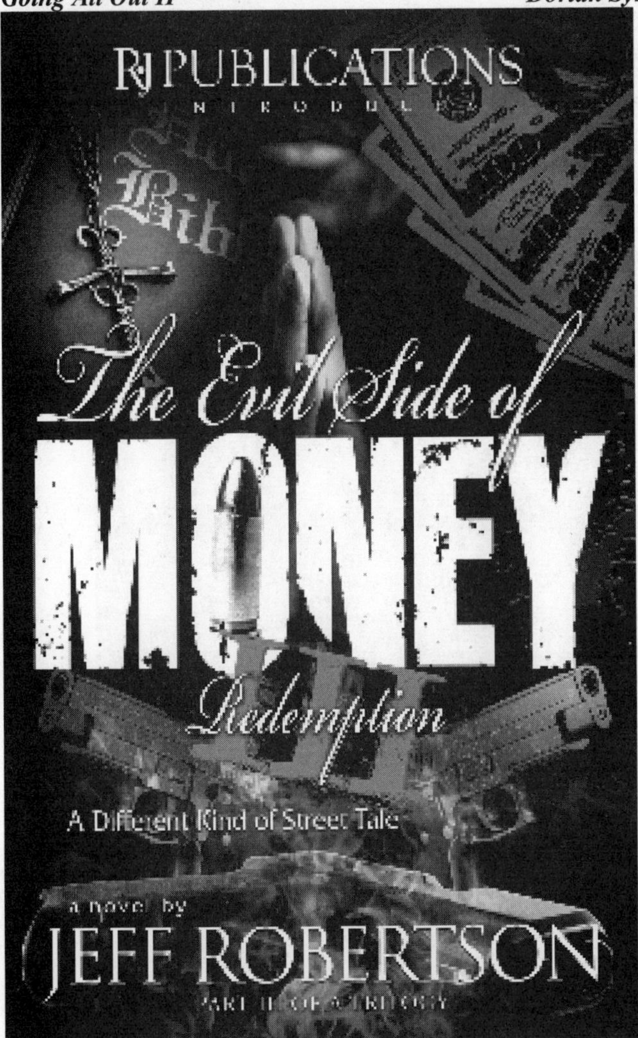

Forced to abandon the drug world for good, Nathan and G attempt to change their lives and move forward, but will their past come back to haunt them? This final installment will leave you speechless.

In Stores!!!

Nafiys Muhammad managed to beat the charges in court and was found innocent as a result. However, his criminal involvement is far from over. While Jerry Class Classon is feeling safe in the witness protection program, his family continues to endure even more pain. There will be many revelations as betrayal, sex scandal, corruption, and murder shape this story. No one will be left unscathed and everyone will pay the price for his/her involvement. Get ready for a rough ride as we revisit the Black Top Crew.

In Stores!!

Dave Richardson is enjoying success as his second book became a New York Times best-seller. He left the life of The Bedroom behind to settle with his family, but an obsessed fan has not had enough of Dave and she will go to great length to get a piece of him. How far will a woman go to get a man that doesn't belong to her?

In Stores!!!

Deon is at the mercy of a ruthless gang that kidnapped him. In a foreign land where he knows nothing about the culture, he has to use his survival instincts and his wit to outsmart his captors. Will the Hoodfellas show up in time to rescue Deon, or will Crazy D take over once again and fight an all out war by himself?

In Stores!!!

The drama continues as Deshun is hunted by Angela who still feels that ex-girlfriend Kayla is still trying to win his heart, though he brutally raped her. Angela will kill anyone who gets in her way, but is DeShun worth all the aggravation?

In Stores!!!

Buck Johnson was forced to make the best out of worst situation. He has witnessed the most cruel events in his life and it is those events who the man that he has become. Was the Johnson family ignorant souls through no fault of their own?

In Stores!!!

When an Ex-con finds himself destitute and in dire need of the basic necessities after he's released from prison, he turns to what he knows best, crime, but at what cost? Extortion, murder and mayhem drives him back to the top, but will he stay there?

In Stores !!!

What happens when someone falls insanely in love? Stalking is just the beginning.

In Stores!!!

Pharaoh decides that his fate would not be settled in court by twelve jurors. His fate would be decided in blood, as he sets out to kill Tez, and those who snitched on him. Pharaoh s definition of Going All Out is either death or freedom. Prison is not an option. Will Pharoah impose his will on those snitches?

In Stores 10/30/2011

Kwame never thought he would come home to find his mother and sister strung out on drugs after his second tour of duty in Iraq. The Gulf war made him tougher, more tenacious, and most of all, turned him to a Navy Seal. Now a veteran, Kwame wanted to come back home to lead a normal life. However, Dirty cops and politicians alike refuse to clean the streets of Newark, New Jersey because the drug industry is big business that keeps their pockets fat. Kwame is determined to rid his neighborhood of all the bad elements, including the dirty cops, dirty politicians and the drug dealers. Will his one-man army be enough for the job?

Coming December 30, 2011

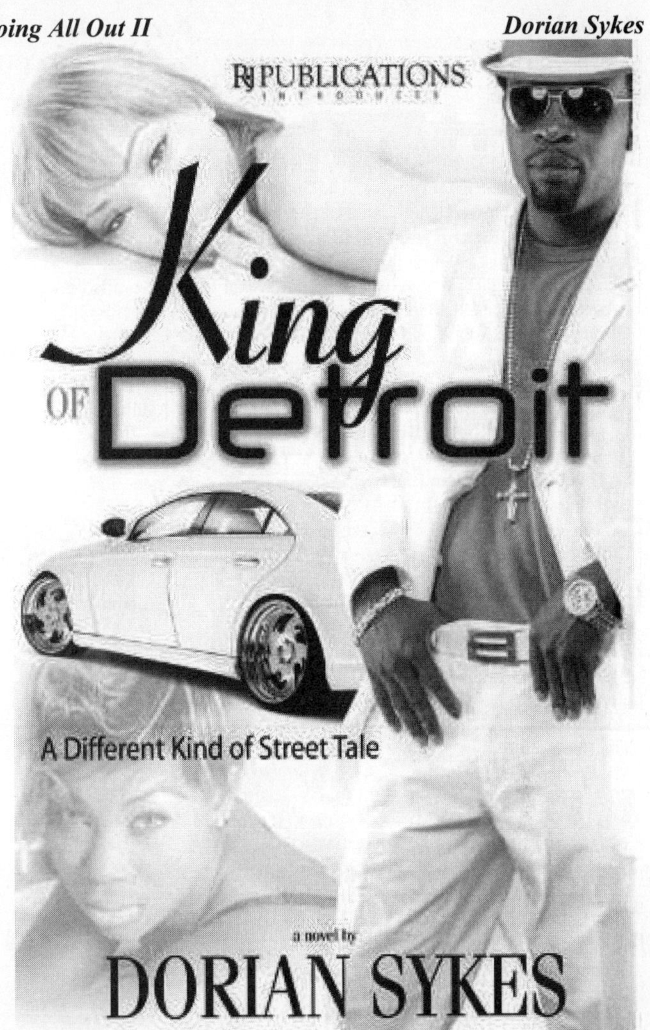

The blood-thirsty streets of Detroit have never seen a King like Corey Coach Townsend. The Legacy of Corey Coach Townsend, the Real King of Detroit, will live on forever. Coach was crowned King after avenging his father s murder, and after going to war with his best friend over the top spot. He always keeps his friends close. Coach s reign as king will forever be stained in the streets of Detroit, as the best who had ever done it, but how will he rise to the top? This is a story of betrayal, revenge and honor. There can only be one king!

In Stores February 15, 2012

PUBLICATIONS
BRINGING EXCITEMENT, FUN AND JOY TO READING